If Teaching Is Your Job

JOHN LESLIE LOBINGIER
AUTHOR OF *The Better Church School*

THE PILGRIM PRESS · BOSTON

CONTENTS

Affectionately Dedicated

to

MARGARET ROBINSON LOBINGIER

The Quality of Our Teaching

Improving the quality of the teaching is the most important task confronting those responsible for the church school.

Equipment is important, and the church needs the best equipment it is able to provide. Curriculum is important, and the responsible church committee must select its curriculum materials with care. More important than equipment and more important than curriculum, however, is the quality of the teaching. To secure the best possible teachers and to help them to become even better teachers is the matter of first concern.

If a church is fortunate enough to have a trained director of Christian education, this director's major task is to help teachers to become better teachers. But so many details of administration crowd in upon directors' time that they constantly face the danger of having no time left for the basic work of improving the quality of the teaching. In any church, large or small, the minister, the superintendent, and the committee on Christian education are responsible for so many matters that they, too, face the peril of merely finding teachers and, having found them, leaving them alone without help in improving their teaching skills.

There are many approaches to the problem of training prospective teachers and continuing the training of those already on the job: summer schools of education, laboratory schools, community training schools, an educational feature at each monthly meeting of the teachers and officers, a workers' library, personal conferences. In addition to such a program for the staff as a whole, each teacher needs to work individually at the task of improving the quality of his or her own teaching. For in this matter, no one has arrived; the best teachers are still learning to teach better.

This little book is written, not with any thought that what it has to say is either new or profound, but with the assurance that the subjects it discusses are the practical questions which average, volunteer teachers are asking, and with the hope that some word here and there, growing out of experience, may prove helpful.

Every church school teacher is confronted with an immediate task — that class session next Sunday! But for the years beyond next Sunday, every teacher needs certain skills, which can be cultivated only by study and practice. Every teacher is thinking about the class he or she is leading, wondering how it differs from younger groups and older groups, and asking what its peculiar needs are. Hardly a church school teacher but, sometime or other, says with knitted brow: " What about this matter of discipline, anyway? " With yearning and uncertainty, thoughtful leaders in the church school review their own efforts from time to time, wondering how they may know whether their teaching is of any value, and what the tests of success really are.

The churches owe a tremendous debt to the host of volunteer teachers in their schools — especially to the volunteers who are not quite satisfied with their present achievement, but who are struggling and striving to be better teachers of their pupils, and for their churches. " If teaching is your job," and if you feel that you have not yet " arrived," this little book is meant for you.

— J. L. L.

Winchester, Massachusetts

I

Next Sunday Is Coming!

If ever we long for better teaching ability it is when we are haunted by the thought that next Sunday is coming!

Even the best-trained teacher continues to receive some of his training " on the job," but with most church school teachers the major part of training comes after the teaching responsibility has begun. This is one of the differences between the day school and the church school: the high school girl who wants to enter the teaching profession, enrolls in a state teachers' college, takes courses with this end in view, includes in her program practice teaching under supervision, and accepts her first position with a background of at least a limited amount of teaching experience, as well as content courses and educational theory. When the church enlists volunteer teachers, however, it may be fortunate enough to secure some who have had that kind of training, but many are without it; the latter may have experiences and qualifications which are in a measure compensatory, but a large number of parents and others who join the church's teaching staff have not enjoyed the opportunities that a teachers' college or a school of education would have given. To them the problem of improving their teaching is pertinent and real. When they think of improving their teaching they are thinking, first of all, of next Sunday's session.

This, then, is the place to begin. How to plan for a class session is our starting point. It may not be the logical approach to the question of better teaching, but if we are realistic in thinking of the majority of church school workers we shall recognize this as the psychological approach.

First of all, we must try to avoid thinking of what we are to do next Sunday as an isolated experience, unrelated to what has gone before or what is to follow. No " lesson " is a thing by itself. It is part of a course and the teacher needs to see the course as a whole before thinking of that one segment of it which we call " next Sunday's lesson."

It is at this point that many a teacher needs to improve. If the course is on the life of Jesus, the teacher should get the sweep of that life before taking up a lesson on one of the parables, or the events of the Last Week, or Jesus' visit to the Temple at the age of twelve. If the course is on the church and the spread of its message around the world, the teacher must try to comprehend it in its entirety before planning a lesson on " Why the Church Reaches Out " or " The Christian Church and Africa." When a leader receives a textbook for the year or quarter, he needs at least to read it through and to understand it as a whole, before attempting to plan for next Sunday.

Not only is next Sunday's work a part of the total course; it may also be a part of a unit within a course. A kindergarten course entitled "A Star Shone," for example, has in it three units, one of which is called " This Is Our Church," with a plan for four sessions to complete the unit: "At Home in Church," " What We Do at Church," " The Minister," and " God Loves a Cheerful Giver." A second-grade course on " Growing in God's World " includes nine units on such themes as " Loving-kindness," " We Keep Christmas," " Many People in Our Country," and so forth. But each unit contains a number of sessions, ranging from four to nine. Sometimes the units within a course are not clearly defined in the teacher's guide, but may easily be organized as such within the teacher's mind. Here, for example, is a three-month junior high course, entitled " The Story the Bible Tells." Although it is not divided into units, the teacher will find it to his advantage to make his own division: (1) Four sessions on what the Hebrews gradually learned about God; (2) Three sessions that show the progress that was made during the reigns of Saul, David and Solomon; (3) Five sessions that help us to see how five of the prophets brought the Hebrews to a truer conception of God; and (4) One session that centers in Jesus.

One does not plan a session without reference to other sessions in the same unit. We plan a given session in relation to what has gone before and what will follow; thus, in a sense, we plan an entire unit — just as a minister who preaches a series of sermons on the beatitudes is bound to think of the whole series, even while he appears to be working on one sermon dealing with a single beatitude.

The inadequacy of any other approach is apparent when we transfer our thought to other teaching fields. What would we think of a teacher of English literature who, by the time of the first class session, had not even read in its entirety the Shakespearean play that his class was to study?

To be specific, I am not ready to begin preparing for next Sunday until I can put the material which is the basis for what I am to do next Sunday into its proper setting, and see it in its true perspective, in relation to what has gone before and what is to follow. If, for example, I am teaching the junior course, *How Our Bible Came to Us*, I shall not be ready to " prepare " for next Sunday unless I have (1) read the entire pupil's book, (2) looked through the leader's guide, (3) tried to do at least some outside reading on such questions as how the Bible came into being, how it came to be " the Book " for Christians, and the story of the many translations. We do not begin by planning a lesson. We begin by doing the preliminary things that give us a grasp of the larger whole and lead us to the point at which we are ready to plan specifically for next Sunday.

WHEN DO WE PLAN NEXT SUNDAY'S SESSION?

Perhaps it is already a little late! In a conference on this general subject the leader asked the question: " When do you begin to plan for next Sunday? " One member of the group responded:

[3]

" Two weeks before next Sunday." Another said: " When I go home on Sunday I take half an hour with pen and paper. While my class session of the day is clearly in mind I make some notes as to points that were left unfinished, problems of the day that need to be kept in mind for the following session, personal needs of pupils that I must remember when planning for the following week. This is just *preliminary* to my planning for the coming Sunday, but it is helpful to have these jottings written down on paper."

This second statement revealed a plan that had proved its value in experience. The first statement also grew out of experience: this teacher had found what many others have discovered — in teaching, in sermon preparation, in connection with a speech to be made — that if one has a subject in mind well in advance, it is surprising to note how many things in one's reading or observation or thinking seem to bear directly on that subject. They fit right in! Some people make a habit of carrying with them a pencil and note-book or blank cards, so that ideas or notes may be written down, to be used when the time for planning comes.

Each must make his own plan, but there must be a plan. The worst plan — or lack of it — is to do nothing until Sunday morning. Begin early, so that there is time for reflection, and so that new material and experiences and observations may accumulate — sometimes from books and everyday experiences and other sources we can clearly identify and sometimes from sources we cannot define.

GENERAL PREPARATION

Before making a specific plan for the class hour there must come general preparation. The church school teacher is fortunate who has in his personal library, in addition to one or more translations of the Bible, (1) a Bible dictionary, (2) a concordance, (3) a Bible atlas. When people let their families know their desires they often find them as ready to give such presents for birthday or Christmas as other articles of only passing value. The church school that has its library for workers should include in it a few basic books of this kind so that volunteer teachers may borrow them or use them at the church. Public libraries often have these books — sometimes used all too little by the church school teachers of the community.

How shall the teacher make his general preparation?

1. *If the lesson is biblical, read the Bible section carefully, making notes.* Are you sure of the meaning of words? the geographical location of places mentioned? the correct pronunciation of each proper noun? the deeper meaning of the passage or the teaching? It is here that books mentioned in the section above prove helpful. Know the facts of the story and the significance of it all.

2. *If there is a pupil's book, read the chapter;* and if it suggests that the pupils do something, do it yourself in advance.

3. *Turn to the teacher's book.* Sometimes a person tries to teach without consulting it at all. It is difficult to know which is worse — to neglect it entirely or to follow it slavishly, even to the point of reading directly from it to the class! It should be used. It has been prepared by a person of considerable experience and contains helpful supplementary material, usually with an outline of a possible procedure for the class period. This is not your outline of procedure, but one that is suggestive. Some parts of it you may want to follow; others you will change. When you make your own outline, you will not copy this outline from the teacher's guide, but, unless you are a teacher of unusual skill and experience, you will find great help in discovering how someone else might teach a lesson on this theme.

4. *Questions for discussion are important.* Of course they will vary at different age levels — very simple questions for primary children, those that reflect differences of opinion or varying beliefs at the high school age level. We cannot leave these questions for the spur of the moment. They need careful thought and the right wording. Write down a few that may prove appropriate.

5. *A story or illustrations tend to lighten up a class session* and give it interest, as well as proving a teaching aid. Some of the best may come out of your own experience or from your reading; you

may also find a suitable one in the teacher's guide. If you begin your general preparation a week or two in advance, good illustrations are more likely to come to mind. Write them down.

Occasionally you may want to use a filmstrip, a slide, or even a short motion picture. Your church may own it. If not, you will have to plan to rent it. Whatever you do with visual resources of this kind, you will want to keep in mind that such material should never be regarded as a substitute for teaching. It is merely an aid in teaching, something that will help to carry out your purpose.

6. *Perhaps your class session will include some kind of activity.* This may be for the group as a whole or for each boy and girl separately. It may be drawing at one age or preparing a code of ethics at another; it may be modeling for younger children or conducting a discussion in an older class; it may be dramatizing or notebook work as a class project, or perhaps a service enterprise. The group may determine its activity, but even so, the teacher must have certain possibilities in mind and what will be required to complete them. There may be suggestions in the leader's guide, but surely there will be others in the teacher's mind. Whatever activity you may list as a possibility, you should be able to answer these questions in the affirmative: (a) Is the activity creative? There is no place in the modern church school for mere busy work; (b) Is it related to the theme of the day? It must help in the teaching of what you are trying to teach; if it does not do this it is a poorly chosen activity; (c) Is it properly graded, so that an activity suitable for primary children, for example, is not given to junior high boys and girls? When we speak of the suitability of group activities we do not forget young people and adults. Their sessions may be made more meaningful by the use of a social distance test or a multiple-choice test; by the introduction of dramatics or role playing, by group discussion or the techniques of group dynamics. (d) Is there variety, so that pupils do not get the impression that there is only one kind that is ever carried on in the church school — *only* drawing, or *only* making blueprints, or *only* writing in the note-book? (e) Has the class had some voice in deciding what the activity is to be, and are you as a

[6]

teacher sufficiently flexible so that you can change from what has been your own first choice if the clear preference of the group is for something else?

7. The leader who has some idea of the public school program for the corresponding grade or department has an asset denied to others. In all sorts of ways the day-school work may be used or assumed, to the enrichment of the church school program.[1]

8. As one thinks about the coming session one will surely consider in advance what materials may well be used. Note them in writing. The list may include a blackboard, a scroll that the church owns, a special picture to be borrowed from the picture file, or materials for certain kinds of creative activity. If you have audio-visual equipment, just what slides or filmstrips will you want?

9. What is the basic meaning of this lesson for my class? This calls for thought. When we begin our planning a week or two in advance, this question may come to mind at odd moments and help us to make our plan with more understanding and insight. The aim of a church school lesson should be more than an expansion of the pupil's knowledge. In addition to this, its purpose may be in terms of friendly attitudes toward people of other cultures and races, or deeper insights into religious truth, or a decision to participate in some church activity, or a serious vocational purpose. When a teacher finds this kind of meaning in "next Sunday's lesson," it helps to throw light on his path of preparation.

MAKING A WRITTEN PLAN

Even the best teacher needs to do this. In fact, the better the teacher, the more likely it is that he will write out his lesson plan —even though it is the less experienced who stands in greater need of the discipline of doing so. The outline may or may not go with one to the class session; that is immaterial. The thing that matters is that one have a plan that is so clearly defined as to be

---

[1]An excellent article on this subject, "Using What They Learn in School," by Bessie P. Erb, has been reprinted from *The International Journal of Religious Education* and is available from the National Council of Churches.

written out, step by step. One may vary from it in actual procedure, according to developments in the session itself. But the written plan suggests a procedure that one may follow, and as such it gives confidence and a sense of direction. There is value in keeping these lesson plans throughout the year, to judge them from time to time for improvement and for variety.

What shall we include in this written lesson plan?

1. *What we hope to achieve in this class session.* We never know whether we have arrived unless we know where it is that we wanted to go. The teacher never knows whether he has realized his aim unless he has a clear understanding of what his objective is. If we cannot state our aim in words, we may question whether we have any clear idea of our goal.

It is quite legitimate for our aim to be in the realm of knowledge, but even then it may be much more than that; it may be knowledge plus. In a missionary lesson on the outreach of the church in the Philippines, the teacher's first aim may be " to lead to an understanding of the work our church is doing in the Philippines, and its significance in the lives of people." In a study of the Bible and how it has come down to us today, the aim of a single lesson may be " to lead pupils to a knowledge of the facts in regard to modern translations of the Bible and to an appreciation of the fact that the newest translations may be nearer to the original manuscripts than older translations which our grandparents used." Any session on a part of the Bible should have factual knowledge as one of its aims. Because we have been emancipated from the idea that our sole objective is the teaching of biblical knowledge, we need not go to the other extreme of introducing the Bible only when we think it will help in the solution of a problem or in throwing light on a life situation. Knowledge is a legitimate aim, and there are times when the sole stated objective for a given session will be in the field of knowledge. Even then we may expect something more.

Our aim may be in terms of attitudes and character development. We may want to achieve something in the area of reverence or gratitude or thoughtfulness. This may not come by talking about these things, but by the experience of worship, the exposure of the pupil to an outstanding personality, and the experience of sharing. The paths that we take to reach our aims are many and varied.

Our aim may be in terms of activity and behavior. We may want to lead toward a decision to engage in an enterprise for the church, or for children of the community, or in world service. A lesson on some aspect of the life and teachings of Jesus may be so pointed as to lead to such an end.

Our aim may be in terms of belief or decision. If our lesson is about God or Jesus or immortality or prayer or the Christian life, we may decide that we would like the outcome to be a clarification of the pupils' Christian beliefs or commitment to the Christian life. That, then, will be the stated aim. In his Lyman Beecher Lectures at Yale, Professor Luccock pointed out that " the aim of preaching is not the elucidation of a subject, but the transformation of a person." [2] Is this not as true of teaching as it is of preaching? Are we not trying to do much more with our pupils than to increase their fund of knowledge?

More often than not it will be impossible to separate our aims into airtight compartments—only knowledge, only commitment, only belief, only attitudes, only Christian character. They overlap. We may state, not a single aim, but two or three which we hope may be realized through the session we are planning. With aims in black and white we shall know the direction in which we want to lead. It may be well to note that the stated aim of one session may be the aim of a group of sessions, for example, all the sessions of a unit.

2. *The materials we expect to use.* These, too, we will list. If we plan to teach with the aid of a blackboard, we list " blackboard, chalk, eraser." If we are to use Bibles in the class and the pupils are not in the habit of bringing their own, we list " Bibles " so that we shall remember to have a supply. If there is a teaching picture we want to use, we note its name so that we shall remem-

[2] Halford E. Luccock, *Communicating the Gospel,* Harper & Brothers, 1954, p. 125.

[9]

ber to get it in advance from the picture file. If ours is a younger class and our activity is to be modeling, we list " plasticene," or if it is to be drawing we list " crayons and manila paper." If ours is a young people's class and we plan to use a true-false test, we list it, to have it ready in advance. If we are to use a filmstrip we shall make a note of it and be sure that necessary preparations are made. For a certain type of session maps will be needed, and these we list also.

3. *How to begin.* The good public speaker spends ample time deciding what his first sentence will be. The effective preacher knows that he will win or lose his congregation in the first two minutes. The church school teacher, too, must recognize the importance of the way he begins.

On the negative side, it is unwise to waste time on matters that are extraneous to the purpose of the class hour. An unfortunate tradition has grown up among some volunteer teachers that there is merit in making a trade with their pupils, as a result of which the first ten minutes will be devoted to football or parties if the next twenty-five minutes are kept for the supposed subject of the morning. Such schemes are both unwise and unnecessary. They are self-defeating devices. The time is all too short as it is, to justify any such waste.

Still on the negative side, taking the offering and marking the attendance book are not good ways to begin. Giving is part of worship, and we may be glad that the trend of recent years has been to include it as an element in group worship. It has not been so easy to free our class sessions from the mechanics of marking attendance. The system is particularly pernicious when three pupils vie with one another — with more or less physical prowess — for the privilege of doing the marking. Most classes are so small that any teacher can remember at the close of the hour the ones who were present. If the class is larger it may have a less experienced assistant teacher who can take this as one responsibility, without having the pupils conscious of the process at all. If the group is very large a system of attendance discs for self-checking may be installed. If the school secretary insists that attendance cards or books must be collected five minutes after the class period begins, it is time for the religious education committee to change the system.

On the positive side, the time to begin is promptly, when the class gathers. The time to begin is as soon as the teacher has attention (but not until then) and before he has lost it.

Still on the positive side, the way to begin is as interestingly as possible and with enough variety so that the beginning is not always the same. From experience every reader can give examples of beginnings that are always the same. But how can we get variety?

One may begin by using a *picture*, if it is just the one that touches the theme of the day. Suppose you decide that Hoffman's " Christ and the Doctors " is the one. Have the picture ready in advance — a good print, properly mounted. Know it so well yourself that you are familiar with the details and the points that you hope will be recognized. Show it and talk about it in conversation, emphasizing important points only when the class members fail to do so. You are using the picture with a purpose; therefore it must serve only as an introduction to what will follow.

The following Sunday a *story* may be made the starting point. It will be chosen because it points in the direction of the day's central theme and it will be told (not read) with as much of the storyteller's art as the teacher possesses.

Especially with younger children there may be a conversation on their experiences of the week, which the skilled teacher will tie together or point up in an appropriate way.

Another time the class session may be opened with a prayer. Some teachers like to begin in this way always; some do so on occasions, when the atmosphere is right or when an opening prayer will create the atmosphere for that particular session.

The beginning may be something a little out of the ordinary. In a course on *How Our Bible Came to Us*, written for use during the fall in which the Revised Standard Version was published, the author starts a session with a riddle:

I have been burned to ashes, but never destroyed.

I am many, yet always one.
I am thousands of years old, but I was made this year.
   — Who am I? [3]

The unusual type of beginning catches the attention and is justified if it leads appropriately into the subject of the day.

On another Sunday one may start by showing something that is outside the experience of the average class member. If it is a world-friendship lesson, this may be an article close to the lives of the people being considered that day. It may be a reminder of a missionary project. If the lesson is about the Bible it may be appropriate to bring a reproduction of an ancient scroll that the church may have in its library; or the teacher may borrow the minister's Greek New Testament or Hebrew Old Testament for the class to look at, not that they can read it, but that they may see more nearly how the words looked as they were originally written.

For a number of Sundays in succession the class may begin its session with a group activity — the making of a Hebrew house of Jesus' time, the informal playing of a story, or preparing a group note-book on the year's program. Such a beginning activity may lead into conversation and discussion and worship.

The important point is that there is value in variety that catches and holds the interest, so that the pattern is not always the same.

4. *The presentation of factual material.* This is a part of almost every class session, whether it be an adult class or a group of children. We are seeking some progress in knowledge as well as growth of other kinds. The teacher must have a clear idea of what this is — facts, information, understandings. The lesson plan will show what this is and how it is to be acquired: through reading, study, discussion; by varied forms of creative activity; with the aid of a map or a blackboard or filmstrip.

Both teacher and pupils may have part in the presentation and the discovery of factual material, and the lesson plan will indicate how and when. The teacher's aim will be, in part, to help his

[3] Grace E. Storms, *How Our Bible Came to Us,* The Pilgrim Press, 1952.

class to know the facts and the meaning of the facts. There may not be any significant character value in a knowledge of the names of the twelve disciples, or in knowing that the Dead Sea is below sea level, or in acquiring facts about Paul's missionary journeys, or in knowing facts about Martin Luther's life and the Protestant Reformation. Still, the one who knows his biblical and church history facts has a basis for an intelligent facing and discussion of many religious questions that will affect his Christian beliefs, his convictions and habits, his attitudes and motives. Some things are not discussable; they are or are not facts. But some known facts are basic to a discussion of significant problems. A class needs to increase its fund of pertinent factual knowledge as a basis for Christian development.

5. *Questions for discussion.* In almost every church school class session we use questions for discussion. Only rarely is the lecture method satisfactory. We need the interplay of minds and the interchange of ideas, and something that will provoke thought on the pupil's part. While the questions themselves will vary greatly at different age levels, the same principle holds true at every age. When dealing with a primary child we shall try to stay on his intellectual level, but we shall use many simple questions to lead him to think and to choose and to discriminate and to form judgments. With older groups our questions will be geared to their level. In adult classes there is a marked revolt against addresses that call for passive listening and a marked increase in the direction of discussion, problem-solving, and group thinking.

If the teacher hopes for discussion he must be ready with questions for discussion — not formal, " all-to-be-answered " questions as in an examination paper — but such as inspire interchange of thought, looking toward group conclusions. The leader needs to write out in advance questions which have been carefully considered. They should be well worded, thought-provoking, and not " yes-or-no " questions. We cannot depend on the inspiration of the moment.

By way of illustration let us take the course of study, referred to above, *How Our Bible Came to Us*, for boys and girls of grades five and six. Chapter 13 is entitled: " Give Me a Bible I Can Read." A teacher at work on a lesson plan might make note of a few possible questions for discussion, such as these:

a. What right has anyone to change the Bible?
b. Why do the translators of the Revised Standard Version think they are nearer the original writers' meaning than is the King James Version?
c. Read Deuteronomy 6: 4-9 (the Shema). The Revised Standard Version says " you walk." The King James Version says " thou walkest." Which do you prefer — and why?
d. When you turn the pages of the Revised Standard Version you see that it seems to have more poetry than the King James Version. Why is this so?

6. *An Activity.* In the younger classes in particular, most class sessions include a place for some activity. A child learns more by doing than by listening, a fact which the wise teacher recognizes and for which he makes provision. In choosing and judging activities for any age one may ask:

a. Is it suited to this age — not too difficult? not too childish?
b. Is it related to the lesson theme—not something extraneous, dragged in?
c. Is it creative — not merely busy work?
d. Is there variety — not always the same type of activity?

An activity in a lesson plan is an integral part of the total plan, and therefore must contribute to the carrying out of the aim for this particular session. This rules out all busy work — handwork of any kind designed merely to keep the child quiet and occupied. A generation ago Christian educators inveighed against " coloring cards." But it is still done! Primary or junior children may model with plasticene, draw freely (not color within an outline) to express an experience or an idea, dramatize a story informally; but always what is done should be a means of achieving the central purpose of the class hour. Junior high or senior high young people may make charts or posters, work on a play, engage in a service activity; but always what they do must be to help in the achievement of the objective for the session. Adults need not be passive listeners for the whole class period. Discussion and tests and role-playing help.

If there is to be an activity, let it appear in the lesson plan, with a clear indication as to the materials that will be needed to carry it out.

7. *How to conclude the session.* If the beginning of a class session is important, its conclusion is equally so. The teacher needs to know how to bring the lesson period to its climax. The way in which the class session proceeds may cause a teacher to forget the prepared plan for its conclusion; but still it remains true that the careful teacher will have in his lesson plan a clear indication of the way in which he *thinks* he may end the session. It is easier to discard a plan than it is to create one on the spur of the moment.

It is the last few minutes that may clinch everything that has been said and done and create an atmosphere that will send the pupil away in an attitude of reverence, or with a new interest and purpose, or with an appreciation of the Christian life, or a new sense of devotion to the church. Because of this possibility a teacher ought to know exactly what the class concluding time is to be. Many a superintendent has ruined a teacher's lesson period by arbitrarily, and without notice, cutting five minutes from the class period. This the superintendent has no right to do.

How may a teacher plan to conclude the lesson period? Variety is important. The same principle that applies to the beginning of a lesson applies to the final moments also; the conclusion must not always be in the same mould. From Sunday to Sunday the character of the conclusion may change, with such possibilities as these:

a. A group decision for action, as a result of the day's study.
b. A group conclusion as to a position agreed upon, an accepted point of view, a kind of code adopted by the members themselves.

c. A memory passage that seems to sum up the thought of the day, and is therefore worthy of being remembered.

d. A few moments of closing worship.

e. An illustration or a story that illustrates the central thought of the class session.

f. A summary by the teacher.

g. A sentence from each member of the group that indicates his understanding of the teaching of the day, or his insight into the meaning of the study, or some purpose to which each may be willing to give expression.

h. A filmstrip or kodachrome slide, carefully selected, that catches the spirit of the hour and visualizes it.

A teacher's thirteen lesson plans for the quarter should indicate many different ways of bringing the class session to a conclusion.

8. *Looking toward the following Sunday.* Somewhere in the session there may be a look ahead toward the following Sunday. It may not come at the end, nor at the beginning, for at either point there is danger of breaking the impressiveness of the lesson period. It may be introduced at different points on different Sundays, but there can always be some connecting link between the theme for today and the way in which we plan to continue next week. This connecting link will be just as real to the pupil as it is in the mind of the teacher, if the work of the year or semester or quarter is a unit in itself. We are not teaching a succession of isolated and unrelated "lessons"; we are engaged in a learning adventure covering a considerable block of time. Throughout this whole period there should be such continuity of thought and activity that what is done today seems like a continuation of what was done a week ago; the whole experience is a continuing process. This suggests one reason why the substitute is unlikely to be as successful as the regular teacher: with the substitute, continuity of thought and experience is impossible; a substitute is more likely merely to "teach a lesson." It is perfectly natural for both teacher and pupils to anticipate the following session, for it is to continue a step farther with what they have

done today. One reason why we often fail to secure much home preparation is that we have already failed at this point of translating a unit of work into an ongoing unified experience, in which interest carries over from session to session.

Another reason why we get no preparation for the coming week on the pupil's part is that we do not expect it. Ask for it. But do not ask for too much. Ask for something specific, about which there can be do doubt, and which seems to the pupil to have some reason to it, because it is related to some point of interest in today's session. If there is something to be read, ask everyone to read it; if there is something to be investigated, ask just one to do it; if there is to be a special activity, a committee may carry it on. It is better not to have everyone assigned to special work every week, but to make assignments occasional. Better than all that has been said, however, is so skilled an approach to the whole teaching task that it will never seem like a teacher making assignments, but rather like a group working together in a search and a discovery, so that outside tasks are simply the things that the members of the group are interested in doing, for which they see a reason, and which they undertake because the whole thing is an enterprise of their own. This is not easy to achieve, but some have achieved it, and it is an ideal toward which to work.

Along with the ideal of making the course of study the pupils' own project, to which they will willingly give some time and attention during the week, there is one other point of importance: church schools that have succeeded, in a measure, in securing the interest and co-operation of the home also succeed, in a measure, in getting parental encouragement for pupils to give a little time between Sundays to study and various kinds of activity. If this eighth item under " Making a Written Plan " for next Sunday's session is to have real meaning, there must be progress in the relationship between church and home, and progress also in the task of making the class itself a co-operative in which pupils feel themselves to be on the inside of the enterprise.

II

When the Class Meets

Sᴜɴᴅᴀʏ ʜᴀs ᴄᴏᴍᴇ! The teacher, we assume, has planned well
in advance. It has not been a hasty, last-minute preparation, but
general preparation for the course as a whole and unhurried
preparation for next Sunday's session. He has even made a careful
lesson plan, showing that he knows how he may begin and how
the class period may continue, step by step.

Now the day has arrived on which teacher and pupils meet.
It is the teacher's opportunity.

1. *Even before the scheduled time for the class session, the
teacher has a responsibility, for there are pupils who come early.*
If there are a number of classes in a department, teachers and
superintendent share this responsibility.

One Sunday morning I visited a church school, by invitation,
" to observe and make suggestions." Arriving half an hour before
starting time, as is my custom when on a mission of this kind, I
looked around to get my bearings. Returning to the primary
department room in a little while, still twenty minutes before
opening time, I found the superintendent at the piano with three
children who had arrived early, all singing together. At five-
minute intervals I looked in again and again. Each time the
number of children had increased. They were using the time
informally to learn new songs. By the time the hour arrived for
the session to begin there were over twenty children around the
piano, eager and happy, intent on the informal group activity of
singing together some songs they already knew and learning some
they had never sung before. As they moved into the slightly more

formal opening of their session, the transition was easy — a continuation, in fact, of a pleasant group experience. Here was a leader who knew how to begin before time to begin.

In another church a primary class made frequent use of the sand table. At this particular time they were making the village of Nazareth with a house such as the one in which Jesus may have lived, the streets, the trees, the animals, the people. As children arrived — before the scheduled time — they went right to the sand table to continue working on their project which they had left the previous Sunday. Their teacher was there, as a member of the group, using these presession moments to advantage. They, too, began before " the time to begin."

Here, too, is a kindergarten class whose five-year-olds straggle in, some unfortunately after the scheduled starting time, but others ten, fifteen, or twenty minutes early. What do they do? Their room is set up with centers of interest and the children make their own choices. Some go to the building corner and start at once to build with blocks. Some go to the reading center where at little tables they find books with fascinating pictures; they sit down and begin at once to look at the pictures and thus, in their own way, to " read " the books. Because the kindergarten teacher is there as the children begin to arrive, everything moves along smoothly and happily.

A junior department has its corner with a browsing table on which are placed a dozen books — written for nine- or ten- or eleven-year-olds, with pictures, and with text in the right-sized type. These are up-to-date books that cry out to be read — such books as *Chand of India, Star of Wonder, Let's Talk About God, Little Miss Callie, Showboat Holiday,* and *Bright Pathways.* The early comers do not need to be asked to go to the browsing table. The books themselves are their invitation.

I am thinking also of a sixth-grade group whose program started with an activity, leading later into group conversation and worship. The class was by itself for the entire session — not with other classes in a department. Each child had his own work material in its own place. Upon arrival — whether that was just

[19]

at the scheduled starting time or fifteen minutes in advance — each one went to the shelves, picked out his own material, and continued his task where he had left it the previous week.

Obviously, in such instances as these, the so-called " disciplinary problem " during the presession period vanishes. Not only that, but the atmosphere created during the five or ten or twenty minutes while children are gathering, before the announced opening time carries over into the session itself. There are no negative values to be overcome or counteracted. The teacher who feels a responsibility for the minutes before the school meets will be gaining extra time, creating a better atmosphere, and making it easier to lead the class when the actual class period arrives. When we think of teacher improvement, looking toward a better class session, we cannot forget what happens before the class meets and before the school or department as a whole meets for assembly or worship or activity.

2. *Before the scheduled time for the class session the teacher has another responsibility — for materials and supplies.* This is not a responsibility that can wait until the first three minutes of the class period. To leave it until then is to waste valuable time and to let the class get out of control. *In advance,* the teacher must be sure that the blackboard is in place — and clean — with chalk and eraser at hand. *In advance* he must look in the picture file, find that picture with which he plans to open the session, and have it where he can pick it up readily. *In advance,* he must see that the map he plans to use is where all can see it. If the plan calls for certain creative activities with the hands, the materials must be ready before the class session — paste, crayons, drawing paper, plasticene, or whatever is required. If certain books are to be used for reference — different Bible translations or an atlas — they must be in place in advance. If a projector is to be used with a filmstrip, it must be set up and ready beforehand. We are not trying to belabor the obvious, but to stress the fact that better teaching is dependent in part upon being ready to begin to teach, with everything in order, as soon as the class session begins.

The preceding paragraph brings us back at once to the problem of equipment. And simple equipment does not require a great expenditure of money. The statement is made above that a teacher might "look in the picture file." Without one we waste money; for excellent pictures are tossed about and lost, whereas it would be an economy to preserve them, and this is easy to do with a place to keep them. There are many ways of making such a file, using the volunteer labor of men of the church — a common practice today in large as well as in small churches. In one church a high, deep shelf was used. Very thin, vertical partitions were put in, so that each space was from two to four inches in width. In this way the pictures could stand upright and it was easy to take them out. Sections were labeled: Early Old Testament, Prophets, Jesus, Nature, Home Missions, Africa, India, Home, Child Life, Our Church, and so forth. Pictures were mounted on stiff construction paper or thin cardboard in uniform sizes, such as 9" by 12" or 12" by 18", the mounting being done on special occasions under the supervision of a person with artistic ability, so that it was neatly done, with pleasing margins. Such a picture-file may be always in process of building, new material being added constantly, and — it is hoped — old and worn material being discarded occasionally. If this kind of inexpensive picture file is in operation the teacher has a place to go for the picture she wants, before the session begins. Many leaders keep their pictures unclassified in drawers. This is inefficient. Pictures should be organized, permanently mounted, and filed carefully.

Materials for creative activities with the hands have also been mentioned. It is easy to find them if they have a fixed place where they are regularly kept. Closets and cabinets are essential. These, too, can be made by volunteer labor, so that there is a cabinet for each class, or a shelf for each class, or a cabinet for each department with materials for any or all the classes, but with a special place for each kind of material.

Browsing tables have been mentioned. These call for something of a library from which a few books are chosen and placed on the tables to catch the attention of earlycomers; for obviously the browsing table will not have the same collection of books month in, month out. Thus bookcases are needed, from which books for the table are taken each Sunday.

Interest centers in the kindergarten have been spoken of. If there is a book center there must be places to keep the books between Sundays, when (as in most cases) the room will be used by other groups. If there is a building center there must be a place to keep the building blocks, within easy reach of the children themselves. An excellent piece of equipment for the kindergarten, to be made by volunteer labor, is a section for coats and hats, three feet high, with a low section on each side for the storage of blocks and other materials.

This is not a discussion of equipment, but of better teaching. The point here is simply that a prerequisite for good teaching is to have all sorts of materials that are to be used within easy access and ready, before the session begins. Where classes are larger than the traditional class, with teacher and an assistant teacher (younger and less experienced), presession responsibility can be divided, so that while one is concerned primarily about the early arrivals the other's chief concern is that the room and the things that are needed shall be in readiness.

3. *The two points just considered may not be separate and unrelated; they may dovetail into each other.* We have spoken of having a plan for children who arrive early, and also of having materials in readiness for the class session. The two may go together. The teacher's plan for earlycomers may be to arrange for the class session jointly with pupils who are there, as a group enterprise. For one of the secrets of successful teaching is found in the ability to bring the pupil into the inside of the enterprise so that he feels that it is his class, that he is helping to make decisions, and that his place in carrying out the enterprise is important. To the three earlycomers the teacher may say: " Let's see if our room is all ready for our class this morning. Is our blackboard clean? Who knows where the chalk is? Do you remember what we decided to do today? Perhaps we can find a picture that will tell us something about that. Let's look for it together! If we were to make our own pictures of this, what would we need? Then let's

find some crayons and paper and have them ready for the whole class when the others come." In some such way teacher or superintendent and early arrivals prepare for the class or department meeting together, and jointly do some of the things that are necessary before the session begins. Sometimes these presession tasks are organized so that responsibilities are fixed in the hands of monitors or committees with such tasks as watering the plants, moistening the sand on the sandtable, caring for chalk and blackboard, arranging tables and chairs, arranging books, and the like.

This kind of approach is suitable for the class period as well as for the presession time. It is merely an example of pupil-teacher co-operation, looking toward better teaching results. The modern pedagogical emphasis is on the democratic process. The pupil-teacher relationship is that of a team, the teacher being the more experienced member of the team. The teacher does not know all the answers, but together they are in a common search for knowledge and in a common effort to map their course and do something together. The relationship is two-sided: of course the teacher will plan what to say and what to do, but such a plan can never be carried out without any thought as to what the pupils will be saying and doing at the same time. The leader will not always say what he had planned to say, nor do what he had planned to do; for pupils and teacher are working together. Even in a presession experience there can be such a thing as " teaching," and it can be by way of co-operation through the democratic method.

4. When the class meets there should be a mood of readiness. The teacher teaches best who gives the impression of being there to stay and who expects the pupils to have the same attitude and manner. This applies to women more than it does to men, for custom demands that men take off their coats and hats and find a place for them. When women keep coats and hats on for the class session the psychological impression is of a temporary relationship — of a person who is anxious to hurry away. The day school teacher removes her coat and hat. When the church school teacher does the same thing the effect is conducive to better teaching.

The same principle holds for pupils. The good church school provides adequate places for their coats and hats, with racks of the right height according to the children's age and size. A boy dangling a cap on his finger is not in a learning mood; nor is a girl wrapped in a heavy coat. Even though the time is only an hour the atmosphere can be that of a school and that of the home.

Readiness is not only outward; it is inward as well. It includes the carefully planned lesson as discussed in the first chapter. This is not necessarily an outline of what the teacher will do at every step, but of what the teacher may do. To have such a plan gives assurance.

To be " ready," a teacher will strive to be free from any sense of slavery to the printed teacher's guide. That is for use at home — not when the class is in session. To read from it is deadly; to keep turning to it for reference is unfortunate.

Being ready means also that one approaches the class period with a consciousness of the real test of a successful session. It is not found in the skill with which one tells a story or the precision with which one holds to a well-outlined lesson plan. The test of success is found, not in what the teacher does, but in what happens to the pupil. Is anything going to happen in the pupil's attitude, in his knowledge, in his actions, in his insights, in his decisions? The teacher who is conscious of this and who keeps in mind such tests of success is on the way toward better teaching.

5. *Can we follow our carefully-made lesson plan?* Whether we can or not, certainly we are in a bad way if we have no such plan. It marks the road that we think we may travel, a road that seems logical to travel, a road that appears to lead to a desired goal.

Still we must be ready to deviate from the plan. Something that we thought would be perfectly clear is not clear; children have an incorrect impression; now is the time to correct this impression. Within the class session a situation arises that reveals an unchristian attitude toward others of another national or cultural group. The time to face it is now. This is a real life situation — not one of the imaginary life situations that are sometimes forced into courses of study, which lack the ring of reality and reflect no problem of this particular group. The situation that arises in your group is a life situation for your particular class and dealing with it now is more important than proceeding to the next point on your outline. From the class there may come a suggestion for a service activity or a fellowship experience that can have real value for all concerned. To follow that through to the point of decision may be more important in building Christian character than to make the pages for a class notebook that you had thought would be an appropriate thing to do.

Deviating from a plan may mean better teaching. It still remains, however, that there has been value in having the plan. Unless these unforeseen situations arise the teacher can proceed with confidence. There is always need to discriminate between unforeseen situations that arise that are clearly important and the irrelevant interruptions with which all of us are familiar, that can take a class off on a tangent into topics of no moment. To permit the latter to pull one off the course is not in the interest of better teaching. Hold to the main course unless it is evident that these alternative suggestions or situations have value from the standpoint of Christian education and growth in Christian living. The unexpected often happens and the good teacher finds it necessary to be adjustable. But one need not be " tossed about by every wind " so that a single pupil may wreck all one's well-laid plans for an effective class hour.

Many published courses of study show every evidence of careful experimentation before being printed. Occasionally such a book will give two outlines for each session: (a) As It Was Planned, and (b) As It Happened. The value of such a record is obvious. To the less experienced teacher it shows how the more experienced teacher meets emergencies and unforeseen situations. It suggests the importance of being ready to modify one's plans when there is sufficient reason. It also shows the value of a basic plan and the desirability of holding to it, in the face of petty and irrelevant attempts on the part of the pupils to wander off into devious paths.

6. *But suppose, when Sunday comes, that this teacher is unable*

to be present! This is regrettable. Illness comes and emergencies do arise, however, and even the most faithful-at-heart must be away. Then there must be a substitute.

Can we expect any such careful planning and " readiness " from a substitute? Certainly it is possible to develop a system that will make the coming in of such a person much less of a break than it often proves to be. The key to this is two-fold: it is to be found, on the one hand, in magnifying the place of the substitute and having him recognize certain obligations; on the other hand, it is to be found in a recognition by the teacher of obligations which he has to the substitute.

We need to enlist competent substitutes — people who cannot assume the responsibilities of regular teaching, but who can and will assume the lesser responsibilities of occasional teaching. Such men and women, however, must have a larger place in the scheme of things than is often the case. Magnifying the place of the substitute need not mean a growing tendency toward absence on the teacher's part. It should mean more interest on the part of more people and, therefore, a more effective church school. With a system of regular substitutes for a grade or department, there is less likelihood that one will take over the class with no expectation other than that of merely filling up the time; this will mean, also, that more people are interested because more are enlisted in the total leadership staff.

The responsibility of a woman substitute, for example, does not begin late in the week, when she hears that the teacher is ill and unable to be present on Sunday. Her responsibility has been going on for weeks before such a call comes to her. For, ideally, she has been an occasional visitor and observer of the class at regular intervals, so that when she meets the boys and girls, she does not come as a stranger. More than this, we have a right to assume that she has been meeting with the other leaders at teachers' conferences. In this way she knows the program and plans of the department, and the course of study of this particular class. A substitute of this kind has recognized her responsibility — a responsibility that is much less than that of the class teacher, but much more than that of a stranger who merely rushes in, on the occasion of a teacher's absence, and uses the half hour with matters that may be extraneous to the class curriculum.

The regular teacher and the superintendent also have an obligation beyond a phone call. It is their obligation to treat the regular substitute as a member of the teaching staff, and to see to it that he or she knows the plans of the class and department and has an outline of its program. The teacher has an obligation to furnish this substitute with the plan for this session that she would have used if she had been able to attend. The regular teacher should be sufficiently resourceful to have a specific project to suggest that will fit in with the ongoing purpose of the course. It is not enough to send a lesson book, without comment.

Some of the newer curriculum materials are suggesting that, in addition to the teacher, each class have " an observer." When such a plan is in operation, and when a school does not have regular substitutes, it would seem logical to have this " observer " take over the class on the rare occasions of the teacher's absence; for this " observer," better than any outsider, knows what has been happening and can more easily pick up the reins. This " observer," moreover, is known to the group, and, therefore, has an advantage that no chance substitute can ever have.

One of the trends of recent years is in the direction of larger classes, with a teacher and an assistant teacher. A class set up on this basis has one of the best solutions to the problem created by a teacher's occasional absence. The assistant is expected to be as regular in attendance as the teacher, helping in various ways each Sunday, and thoroughly familiar with the class program, the aims of the year's work, and the various activities of the group. No one knows better than the assistant how the session was brought to a conclusion last Sunday and how to carry on from that point. When a teacher must be away, there is no more logical substitute than the assistant, if there is one. Under her leadership the class period is likely to move along smoothly, without any feeling on the pupils' part that they are being led by a person whom they would regard as a substitute.

III

The Teacher

Better teaching calls for better people to do the teaching. By " better " we refer not only to everyday " goodness," but also, convictions and insights, attitudes and understandings.

1. *The teacher in the church school must believe in the importance of Christian education in the church.* Is this not obvious? By no means. Are there not many serving in this capacity with only a half-hearted belief that the church school makes any difference? The fact that the Sunday School enrollment passed the 35,000,000 mark in 1953, increasing three times as much over the previous year as did church membership,[1] does not prove that all those who hold positions of leadership in it are thoroughly committed to its value. There are still some who teach from a sense of duty to a long-established institution, or because they have been urged and can hardly continue to give a negative answer.

I would not beg anyone to teach in the church school. It is better off without the help of people who are not committed to the idea. For the teacher in the school of the church ought to be a believer in the institution in which he is working. He ought to like it and think it important. He ought to believe that through it children and young people and men and women will have something added to their lives that will enrich them and make them more complete. Unless one is convinced of the value of group worship and of training in the elements of worship; of Bible study and a study of the church and of Christian living; of a recognition of the significance of Christmas and Easter and other great seasons of the church year; of the exaltation of idealism and the highest

[1] See the *Year Book of American Churches, 1955.*

Christian values over lesser standards of everyday life; of Christian service and Christian vocation; of association with others in a company among whom moral and spiritual and religious life is exalted; — unless one is really convinced that such values are important and that they can be advanced through the church school, one had better not accept an invitation to be a teacher, but remain content to fit into some other niche in the life of the church.

Do we not have a right to expect of the church school teacher something of the same enthusiasm that we find in the real artist who paints his picture because of an urge to express himself on canvas, not because of any financial return that may come. Or the true musician who is engrossed in his music because he loves it? Often we find church school teachers with no less enthusiasm for their avocation. It is important to them. They believe in it.

2. *The teacher in the school of the church must be one who measures up well as a person.* Obvious though this may seem, it is of such paramount importance that no one would dare write of the teacher without stressing this point.

However hard a worker, however skillful, however up-to-date in methods, the matter of prime importance is still the kind of person the teacher is.

Do others see him — or her — as a person of Christian faith? This has no relation at all to the teacher's theological point of view — liberal or fundamentalist or middle-of-the-road. The question is, does this leader have a faith that marks him as a genuine Christian — a person of undoubted Christian profession, conviction and purpose?

Do others see in the teacher a loyal churchman who supports the church, attends its services, and participates in its life and activities to such an extent that clearly the church occupies a large place in his life and concern?

Is the teacher regarded as a good citizen, with a well-rounded interest in worthwhile activities and causes of the community and of the world? A religious leader must not be narrow and parochial in his interests — even the narrowness of no interests at all beyond his own church! The humanitarian and cultural and educational causes that press upon us are so many that it behooves us to respond to some of them and to be a participant in activities beyond the walls of home and church.

Do his neighbors and the people of the community think of this person as a man or a woman of exemplary life, with the common everyday qualities of sincerity and honesty and virtue and kindness? We are sometimes distressed by the fact that when an active church worker happens to get into trouble with the law, the newspapers seem to take delight in such headlines as: "Sunday School Teacher Charged With Forgery"! Perhaps it is a compliment to the church that such things are recognized as so inconsistent with the life of a churchman that their occurrence is news.

Do others see in this teacher a person of real convictions on social issues, for which he is willing to stand, even against the prevalent social practice of the community? At a time when gambling is eating into the fabric of our society, is he the kind of person who is counted against it? At a time when liquor is admittedly so great a factor in the direction of crime, is this teacher recognized — by personal practice and by influence — as completely a force against the liquor traffic?

Even the teacher's manner in the class-room is reflected in the members of the class. The way teachers act determines in large measure the way pupils will act. Nervousness, irritability, being "on edge" — these qualities are so contagious that pupils can catch them from a teacher; whereas poise, calmness, and an easy, pleasant manner are also likely to be reflected in the attitudes of the members of the class.

The influence of the teacher depends largely upon what he is, quite apart from any fund of knowledge or any ability in class-room methods. Particularly is this true in the teaching of religion. While this in no way minimizes the importance of adequate training in subject matter and in teaching method, it does point up the fact that better teaching always calls for better persons as teachers.

3. *The church school teacher ought to have convictions as to his reasons for teaching religion.* Such teaching is for the purpose of bringing about some kind of results, and we ought to know the results for which we are looking. I may not be looking for results identical with those for which you are looking, but both of us need convictions of our own as to the results we hope to see.

For one thing, I want the pupils I teach to be *biblical literates,* and literate also in some other areas of knowledge. Do not discount knowledge in itself. Because one can possess a great fund of knowledge, and at the same time be a scoundrel, is no reason to discount knowledge. This is not our only reason for teaching, but it is one. The world — even the Christian community — is too full of biblical illiterates. As a result of our teaching, pupils ought to have a knowledge of the Bible, of the history of the church, of the story of the outreach of the church.

I want the pupils I teach to be *taking their places in the life of the church,* in ways that are appropriate to their age and development. The primary child may have as great a sense of " my church " as his parents have, although the manifestation of this feeling will be very different. The sense of possession and the feeling of " at-home-ness " in the kindergarten child, the church school loyalty of a boy in the junior department, the desire on the part of a junior high pupil to become a member of the church — all result from the right teaching process.

As a result of my teaching efforts I hope to see in my pupils *more Christian attitudes* than would have been possible if they had never been in the church school, so that they reflect increasingly the characteristics of the beatitudes and the qualities of life that the Sermon on the Mount exalts. I want to see more honesty, reverence, gratitude and thoughtfulness, and more friendliness for others — whether or not these others are of the same racial or national or social group as themselves.

I want the pupils I teach to develop *a sense of wonder* in the world — a sense of something higher than themselves — a sense of God. In the face of the secularism and the materialism of the day, can our church school teaching cultivate worship as a natural experience and the consciousness of a Power in the world greater than ourselves?

Through my Christian teaching I believe that my pupils ought to understand *the Christian way of life* better and practice it more and more in their everyday relationships. This has to do with life in the home, at the school, at the church, in the field of sports, in pupils' part-time jobs, in their social activities. We speak of the way of Jesus as something that has relevance to life in the twentieth century. Do we believe that we can expect to see that way of life lived more truly as a result of our feeble teaching efforts?

I have a conviction that the teaching of religion has value in that it is carried on under influences of Christian idealism and in a group in which it is expected that religious values will be exalted. When pupils come to feel at home in such a group, unconsciously they are influenced by it — not simply by what the members have attained but by the ideals that are ever kept before them.

I also want the pupils I teach to develop a *sense of Christian vocation.* Whether or not the matter is made a point of discussion, pupils do a great deal of thinking along the line of their life work. We want the decisions they make to be on the basis of Christian principles. Of equal importance are their avocational habits and ideas. How do they spend their spare time? What do they do when they do as they please? What will their avocations be twenty years from now? These are results that may come indirectly; they may not be talked about; but still the teacher's influence may count in these directions.

We shall not have better teaching unless teachers know why they teach. Your reasons may not be identical with these that have been suggested; and what are yours today may not be yours tomorrow; but always to have some reasons that seem important to you is essential.

4. *The teacher must know what teaching is.* One evening I spoke to a group on the subject: " When the teacher teaches, what do the pupils do? " Somebody said: " What don't they do!"

Of course the logical answer is: " When the teacher teaches, the pupils learn." By that we mean (if we give a broad interpretation to the word "learn") that the pupils gain new understandings, new insights, more information, changed attitudes, new points of view, new purposes. All this and more is a part of learning. But if the pupils are not learning in some such sense, then the teacher has not been teaching. There may have been plenty of talking, but no teaching.

For teaching is a two-way process. It is not just talking, which may be a one-way process. If the teacher just talks and nobody else participates in any way, there is probably no learning. And if there is no learning there is no teaching.

Teaching is helping pupils to learn. Learning to teach better is learning better how to help pupils to learn. Thus to be a better teacher one must be a better learner. The good teacher is a good learner.

The classroom differs from the church congregation. The preacher's sermon may or may not be a teaching experience, but even when it is, it is not a two-way process to the extent that the class-room is — or ought to be. For in the sermon there is no give-and-take, no interchange of thought, no clearing up of difficulties, no activity beyond mental concentration on the part of the hearer. While the sermon has some values that the class-room cannot have, the class-room has possible values that the sermon cannot have. The church school teacher loses if he copies the method of the sermon and turns a lesson period into a long talk — a miniature sermon.

Because there is no learning without participation, there is no teaching without opportunities for pupil participation. Such participation may be of various kinds. It may be reliving the experiences of others, which we call dramatization; if so, the teacher requires skill in this field. It may be manual activity — making things with the hands that will help pupils to understand better and to visualize more clearly; if so, the teacher requires additional skills in order to be a leader and guide. It may be keeping records of group activities, or of things learned, or of decisions made; if so, the teacher must know something of note-book making and note-book keeping in order to be really the more experienced member of the group. It may be thinking problems through and talking them over with others in the class; if so, the teacher needs skill in the conduct of group discussion and in the art of stimulating thought and drawing out different points of view.

There would be no point in the teacher learning such skills as those just suggested, if teaching were just talking. Teaching being what it is, however, the learning of such skills becomes essential. Any method or aid is important if it helps the teacher to co-operate with the pupils in a common search for more knowledge, better understanding, wise decisions, and suitable action. There is not much teaching going on in any class in which pupils are mere passive listeners.

5. *The teacher must know the lesson — plus.* That class is fortunate whose teacher is clearly a learner. We never complete our education, no matter how much we may use that expression to describe graduation from this institution or that; we are always in process of going on with our learning; if not, we have reached a pitiable state.

It is common to speak of the newer (but really not so new) relationship between teacher and class in terms of a group searching for truth, the only difference between teacher and pupils being that the former is a more experienced member of the learning group. The search is a common enterprise; the teacher — like the pupils — has more to learn. All have the open mind and the learner's attitude. But still the leader must go far beyond the other members of the class, however ideal that class may be.

We take it for granted that the teacher aims to be something of an expert in the subject matter of the course. If the study is of the early disciples, he must be familiar with what the Bible tells about them and also what the course book has to say. But this much is expected of the more alert pupils. With the teacher there is a " plus "; and it is this " plus " that helps to differentiate the drab teacher from the interesting teacher — with sparkle. The latter has used an historical geography to the point of familiarity with the places where these disciples worked; he can go to the blackboard and quickly outline the Mediterranean coast and the Jordan River; having read a book on the home life of the Jews in New Testament times, he can shed light on the discussion at various points. If the study is on the Bible and how it has come down to us through the years, this teacher with a " plus " has gone beyond the teacher's and the pupil's books and knows something additional in regard to the story of the translations; he can talk about scrolls and copyists and translations into eleven hundred tongues and the many different versions in our own language; he is familiar with the story of the Revised Standard Version and why this newest version is really the oldest; he has read about the " Vinegar Bible," the " Breeches Bible," the " Ears to Ear Bible," the " Placemaker's Bible," and many others and can lighten up the session with interesting bits of information. This kind of teacher has read about the Syrian shepherds who chased a goat into a cave near the Dead Sea, south of Jericho, in 1947, and there found old jars in which were scrolls containing parts of Isaiah and Habakkuk and dating back to the first century; he can therefore tell his class something about how Bible books were written, and copied, and preserved, and lost, and found — and how old manuscripts bring us nearer to the original writings. Having read a little on biblical archeology, he can tell his class something that sheds new light on a Bible story or corroborates that story in a new and interesting way. If the study has to do with the outreach of the church in India and Pakistan and Ceylon, this alert teacher goes beyond the student's book and the teacher's guide and reads the Friendship Press study book for this particular age, with its story and background material.

This kind of teacher knows his lessons — plus. It is the plus quality in his way of doing things that adds to the interest of the group, because the teacher can add interesting sidelights. One of the marks of a good teacher, then, is that he not only knows his subject, but knows new and interesting aspects of it, and shows that he believes in it by giving evidence that he has explored in many related fields and has brought out unusual treasures to share with his class. In him the class members see an enthusiast for the theme of study.

This kind of teacher, who is himself a learning and growing personality, furnishes an environment in which pupils will grow, and in which they will see new meanings in Bible study and new meanings in life. A class is not likely to stagnate in the atmosphere of a leader who shows no signs of stagnation.

6. *The good teacher believes in the democratic approach.* This is not the easiest way to teach, nor the quickest. For that matter the democratic way in civic life is neither the quickest nor the cheapest; but still we are strong for maintaining it.

The quickest procedure is for the leader to tell the members of the group what they ought to know — to talk, to lecture, and to keep the members of the class quietly on the receiving end. But in this there is no " give and take," no interchange of thought, no discussion with viewpoints challenged and defended. A recent writer on teaching expressed the belief that there are fewer good teachers today than a century ago. If this is true in colleges and universities, it may be because there are more scholars, research specialists, scientifically trained professors than in previous generations; and these are not necessarily the best teachers. Shifting quickly to the field of religious education, some excellent Bible scholars are poor Bible teachers, especially with children and young people; some missionaries are not as good teachers of missions as certain others without their rich background of experience. This may be a comfort to church school teachers who are conscious of their own limitations, but let them not think that the reverse is necessarily true and that because they are neither missionary nor biblical experts they must be excellent teachers in these fields! Even a teacher who is conscious of his limitations as far as the mastery of his field is concerned may cultivate the democratic interchange of thought with his pupils; for this is basic in good teaching.

When we study Jesus as a teacher we are impressed by the way in which he drew people out. He asked questions and others asked questions of him. He provoked thought in others and teaching became a two-way process. Gilbert Highet says that the queerest thing about the teaching of Socrates is that we do not know exactly *what* he did teach; that what we do know is *how* he taught.[2] He used conversation and he used questions, and the whole procedure was one of stimulated thinking, give and take, teacher and student thinking things through together.

When the procedure of a certain denominational agency in the field of social action was being discussed, someone said: " I don't want any group to tell me what my viewpoint should be on a disputed issue; but I do want these representatives of mine to furnish such helps as will make it easier for me to determine my own point of view." It is something like that with the church school teacher: ideally he does not tell his pupils the answers when they are considering the Christian point of view toward life, but, by means of democratic procedures and in the give and take of the group, he tries to make it easier for them to decide for themselves.

The teacher who believes in this democratic approach is bound to have respect for the opinions and statements of everyone. The contribution that each one makes will be received and weighed — however simple, wrong, or off-the-track it may appear — if it is made in sincerity. When such contribution comes from a cut-up who is trying to be smart, the teacher is right, of course, in treating it and the pupil as they deserve.

One who is convinced of the wisdom of the democratic approach works toward group decisions and welcomes them — as to the class viewpoint on debatable issues and as to procedures for their own program. This is more difficult than for the leader to decide, but it is more significant, for it is part of the pupils' religious education. On the leader's part, it requires skill, poise and patience. Those who talk of group dynamics and group-centered leadership rightly stress the fact that the responsibility for making decisions is that of the group itself. Even in a church school class this is the ideal toward which the teacher works.

[2] Gilbert Highet, " Great Teachers and Their Pupils," in *The Art of Teaching,* Alfred A. Knopf, 1950.

How does this apply to controversial issues? In the field of theology and biblical interpretation there are bound to be contradictory opinions in any church. Similarly, ethical questions and matters of behavior are also controversial. And in the church school classroom there may come up questions on race relations, international relations, the freedoms which the Constitution guarantees us all, and whether these freedoms are ever in danger. Must not the teacher be guided by the same democratic ideal and see to it that both sides of controversial issues are presented? And that he himself is sufficiently unbiased to give conflicting views a hearing? And that even if parents criticize reports that come from such a class procedure, the teacher will feel secure in the belief that Christian education, like general education, must practice the way of freedom and help learners to discover truth for themselves and come to their own decisions?

7. *The good teacher, while always remembering to " act his age," is able to enter into comradely relations with the members of his class.* One sometimes observes a sense of " togetherness " in a teacher and a class group that cannot easily be defined but which is a powerful factor for success. The one is always the leader and the others are always the pupils, but still they seem happy to be in one group. They seem to learn *together* — not one on a pedestal while others are down below. While an air of freedom, ease and friendliness prevails, the teacher never lets the reins get out of his hands. Such a situation can never be unless one really likes people—including the members of one's class, whether it is a class of men and women or junior high's or kindergarten children.

Some teachers who seek this sense of comradeship are not content with having a mimeographed statement on the year's program sent to each pupil in September. They send in addition a personal letter to each member of the class, hand written, that has nothing to do with the work of the year but which is really personal. And this friendly contact continues throughout the year.

No teacher will cultivate this sense of comradeship without a sense of humor. This certainly does not mean that he will be telling jokes constantly. Deliver us from that! It certainly does not mean that one will ever resort to satire or let it appear that he is ever making fun of a member of the group. Where there is a sense of humor, class and teacher can sometimes laugh together. Laughing together helps to link them together, and the better they are linked together the more readily do they learn together.

A sense of humor must be two-sided. The teacher of a junior-high class in the day school was fond of telling stories or experiences that to her were funny; sometimes the class responded as she wanted them to, while at other times their response was merely one of blank looks. One day she said to them: " You must be English. You know it takes an Englishman twenty-four hours to see the point." The next day, at the corresponding moment (at a signal from one member, of course) the entire class suddenly burst out into hilarious laughter! The teacher looked at them in astonishment. One boy stood up and said, " Miss Brown, you see we're like the English. We've just seen the point! " That was her chance to laugh with them and admit that they had come back at her completely. Instead she kept the boy who had spoken up for an hour after school!

There is no such thing as a sense of humor if it moves on a one-way track.

8. *The teacher must know how pupils learn.* One who knows this, knows something about the mental capacity of the age he is teaching and, more than that, of the mental capacity of the individual child within the group. We do not teach algebra in the third grade; neither do we teach the book of Revelation to a third grader in the church school. I once heard a leader urging kindergarten children to make more generous contributions " in order that the church might meet its denominational apportionment "! She must have gotten her speech mixed up with the one she intended to give to the adult class or to the high school department. Our curriculum writers are chosen partly on the basis of their knowledge of the age for which they write; for they must not underestimate, nor must they overestimate the pupils' capacity. The teacher is confronted by the same problem: he cannot expect

his pupils to learn, except within the framework of their own mental capacity.

Pupils learn more readily when they have the right motivation and when what they do is based on interest. Years ago, John Dewey, in his " Interest and Effort in Education," taught us the importance of building on interest that already exists in order to increase effort and to lead out into newer and larger interests. The good teacher must be aware that the child learns in this way; he must know something of the life of this particular child and of the group to which this child belongs. Although we begin with present interests, we do not stop there. The good teacher is never content with merely seeing pupils develop new interests. From an interest in reading, they may be led to a new interest in reading the best; from interest in people, they are led to an interest in a Person who exemplified the best in life: from an interest in vocation, they are led into Christian vocational choices; from an interest in a group of friends in a church school class they are led toward an interest in the church and its mission in the world.

Pupils learn also by what they do. This is old doctrine as far as the great teachers are concerned; but average teachers have barely begun to translate precept into practice. The better teacher believes in the doctrine and puts it into practice. What one does has a more lasting effect than what one hears. The good leader, therefore, engages pupils in worthwhile activities. The second-grade child who uses plasticene to build a house such as people lived in during Bible times or the third-grader who makes a Palestinian village on the sandtable has a background for biblical study that the mere listener does not have. The junior class that studies the parable of the Good Samaritan by dramatizing it informally has so relived the experiences of the characters in that story that it has left on their lives an indelible impression. The junior high class that engages in a study of other faiths and other denominations, and divides into groups to make visits — one to a Friends' meeting, one to a Jewish synagogue, one to a church of another racial or language background — has an understanding and appreciation of at least one other faith or church that could never come merely from much talking on the teacher's part. The young people whose Christian education includes service activities, and who actually assist in the children's program of a social settlement on Saturday mornings, develop a sense of Christian mission that could never come from a class discussion. The good leader puts into practice the belief that pupils learn by doing.

Pupils learn also by the process of thinking — thinking for themselves. Socrates made people think. He kept raising questions and challenging viewpoints until his pupils thought their way into their own points of view. The church school study may be on gambling or belief in God or the value of the church. One kind of teacher talks much and gives the answers. Another kind of teacher stimulates the thinking of the pupils and challenges their conclusions so that they do their own thinking and make their own discoveries. The good teacher knows that although this is a slower way of conducting a class, it is a surer way of learning.

It is also by making choices and decisions that pupils learn. We go through life making choices, some of which are in the realm of the moral, the ethical and the spiritual. There is " a high way and a low," to quote John Oxenham, between which we must decide. In the church school such decisions are made on everyday moral questions between the way of life that we call Christian and some lesser way. Pupils learn much more through choices that they make than through any teacher's exhortations.

9. *The good teacher strives for a growing understanding of the pupil in all his relationships*. Books help, and the teacher turns occasionally toward a book that touches upon the psychology of the age he is teaching. Many a book that would not be listed under the label of psychology is equally helpful as it shows through story and action how one of that age behaves and what he is like. *There's No Place Like Home* and *It Runs in the Family* by Ellenwood and *Seventeen* by Tarkington come in this category. Reading of this kind helps a teacher to see a little deeper into the feelings, tensions, interests and struggles of a child or a youth of the age he is teaching.

He goes farther and tries to understand his pupils not merely through books but in their actual life situations. First, there is the home. The teacher ought to know the home from having been in it, and if his acquaintance extends to the parents as persons he has a great asset. Then there is the school. The growing teacher tries to know something of the school and its program. What are these boys and girls studying during the week? What units of work does their curriculum include? Something done on Sunday may be linked up with the weekday program without having anything said about the relationship. There is also the area of play and recreation. If mine is a high school class it behooves me to know something about the football schedule of the fall or the ones who play on the basketball team. If mine is an elementary school group, what are the things these children like best to do when free to do what they choose?

The good teacher must also remember the pupil's environment, for it is a big factor in forming his character and directing his interests. Who, more than the church school teacher, should be concerned as to playgrounds, pool-halls, movies, places where liquor is sold, the library, places where gangs hang out — forces for both good and evil in the community. At a time when juvenile delinquency has become a menacing problem, the teacher who thinks of his task in terms of achieving the objectives of Christian education senses a responsibility beyond the walls of his classroom in the community as a whole. As a good citizen and a Christian teacher, he takes his part in community affairs.

For we recognize that there are teaching forces in the lives of pupils, other than those that are under the direction of the men and women called teachers. Some are for good and some are for ill. The better teacher is the kind of person who is sufficiently aware of life in his community to be concerned, and sufficiently concerned to participate in efforts toward a wholesome environment.

The growing teacher also tries to know something of the pupils' inner life and feelings. He wishes he might have much more sensitivity than most of us possess, in being able to understand the problem child or the one whose attitude and behavior deviate from what we regard as normal.

In recent years, more than ever before, our curriculum planners have been calling in the psychiatrists and psychologists for assistance. This is reflected in the suggestions we find in teachers' guides, with many references to the child with a sense of insecurity, to the pupil who is lonely, to the boy with a feeling of guilt, to the girl with a sense of rejection. These are among the situations with which psychiatrists deal constantly. They often see these feelings as related to parental treatment or trace them to other aspects of the child's experience. Like a doctor who deals with causes, not symptoms, these specialists try to discover the causes and deal with them.

The teacher must know enough about such matters to recognize the possible roots of abnormal or unusual behavior. This is an area, however, in which the average volunteer teacher is no specialist and, therefore, needs to use great caution.

One thing a teacher can do is to love and befriend the child, even though that child's inner tensions may make him seem less lovable and less friendly. How often we are reminded that however great may be our disapproval of certain *actions*, we must be careful not to show disapproval of a pupil *as a person!*

Still another thing this teacher may do is to keep this child from being too introspective, by guiding him into interesting and significant activities, so that the doing of worthwhile things in the group will crowd out the sense of loneliness or rejection.

It is important, also, that the teacher's approach be positive, not negative. To some of us, the weakness of certain courses of study is at this point; the life situations, real or imaginary, are so often entirely negative — the wrong acts of a child and unethical behavior. This is not the way to root out evil. If we keep harping on problems and on the negative, we may make problem children out of normal children.

Using a course of study with this approach, the inexperienced teacher is in danger of too much generalization. If there is one lonely child, this does not mean that all children in the class are lonely. Because one has a marked sense of insecurity, we have no reason to generalize and to assume that every child in the group has a marked sense of insecurity. Because one seems to have a deep sense of guilt, we must not treat all in such a way that they begin to think they have the same inner feeling. The danger is that this emphasis in a course, reflecting the problems of the occasional child, will be misused by a teacher who generalizes to the point of putting all of his children in the same category. The problem of the occasional child can best be dealt with individually, not in the class session.

The child who needs help ought to have it. But it is dangerous for the average teacher to attempt to pose as a psychologist or a psychiatrist. What this teacher can do is to be a true friend, to stress the positive, to guide a child into wholesome activities. Having done this, however, suppose he finds that the pupil still seems to be a problem child, with real inner conflicts and tensions? At such a time a teacher had better not be among those who rush in where angels fear to tread. Instead, seek help. So many theological seminaries are giving training today in counseling and pastoral care, that more ministers than ever before are in a position to give assistance; perhaps your minister is one who can help. On the other hand, a conference with parents may seem desirable; and, if the case warrants, these parents themselves may decide to seek the assistance of a psychiatrist, or a child guidance clinic, or perhaps of a doctor — for some situations are basically problems of physical health, not mental health. The average teacher, however, had better not get beyond his depth, but confine himself to doing what he is equipped to do.

IV

Skill in Leading a Discussion

ONE who is to teach in the church school must acquire certain basic skills, such as skill in guiding conversation and leading a discussion, skill in telling a story well, skill in the use of various forms of creative activity, skill in steering the class in its group projects and service enterprises.

The first teacher training text I ever used covered the Bible, church school organization, child psychology, and pedagogy — all in forty sessions. Perhaps the author did not intend it so, but it appeared as if one was to learn how to teach by memorizing the list of points on teaching; that one was to learn how to tell stories well by learning the steps outlined in the book. It is not so simple. The text is merely a guide to experience, for we learn to teach by teaching, and we learn how to lead a discussion in the process of discussion leading. All that a book can do is to give a little assistance so that one may enter into actual teaching situations with certain techniques in mind that others have found satisfactory, and be aware of pitfalls to be avoided.

The laboratory school has been a great boon to Christian education, but even it cannot do everything. Even the observation-practice school, with its opportunity to observe good teaching, its time for practice teaching, and its periods of evaluation, has too crowded a program to include what needs to be included in the development of basic skills. It must be supplemented by actual experiences in the acquisition of the particular skill in question. Thus there is great advantage in a workshop in creative activities, a course in storytelling with practice and criticism, and a course in discussion-leading as prerequisites to enrollment in the ordinary brief laboratory school.

It is encouraging to find an occasional " Skill Shop " set up as a variation of the Community School of Religious Education, at which teachers themselves may learn how to letter, to draw, to engage in informal dramatization, to tell stories, to make a diorama, and so forth, so that they may be better teachers and may know how to lead their pupils into creative experiences.[1]

One may serve as assistant teacher and gain practice in these fields under a capable and experienced teacher. Moreover, since so much leadership training in religious education must be " on the job " rather than while one is preparing to teach, it is necessary that one improve one's skill in these fields in normal teaching situations.

The average teacher, therefore, needs the help that can come from books, from the workshop in which major skills are learned, and from experience itself. In this chapter we begin with the need for greater skill in leading a discussion.

The ability to lead a discussion calls for a certain point of view. The good discussion leader must believe that *teaching is more than telling*. He knows that pupils learn, in part, by the give and take of group discussion, by having their viewpoints challenged and having to defend their positions.

The good discussion leader realizes *the importance of pupil participation*. When people have a chance to express themselves, they not only enjoy it, but they are also crystallizing their own points of view, weighing them against other viewpoints, and thus opening the door for real learning. The discussion method is miles removed from the forty-minute lecture concluding with "Are there any questions? " In a well-conducted discussion, teacher and pupils are working together toward a conclusion or a decision. The procedure itself stimulates thinking, which is a basic aim of the good leader.

The class session is a different kind of experience from the sermon. As part of a worship service the sermon may do some-

[1]A brief account of such a Skill Shop is found in *The International Journal of Religious Education,* January, 1955: "A Skill Shop in St. Louis " by Paul Rains.

thing emotionally that a class session rarely does. Even when a minister says that he wants his pulpit to be a teaching pulpit and builds his sermon on that theory, it still lacks the give and take of good teaching technique. I am thinking of a church in which it was the custom for a number of years to have a forty-minute forum and discussion, following the worship service, in which people had the opportunity — under the chairmanship of a good discussion leader — to discuss the sermon, take issue with the minister, ask him for clarification on some point, and enjoy the give and take of group thinking on the theme of the morning discourse.

The good discussion leader has learned *how to disagree in good spirit* and has learned also how to help the members of his group to disagree in the same good spirit. He knows that sincere differences of opinion are wholesome, and that to lead his class to express their differences without getting emotionally upset is a part of good religious education.

Even the arrangement of the room and the seating are important factors in group discussion. When a discussion group is announced as meeting " in the sanctuary " or " in the chapel " the hearers have no feeling of its being a real discussion group. When people sit in rows, in pews, in an atmosphere associated with quiet meditation, they are not in the perfect mood for a discussion group. The church parlor is better, with people at ease and in an air of informality; or a classroom; or any other room in which members may gather somewhat as they would in a person's living room, or perhaps about a table—with no one facing another person's back. Such an arrangement lends itself much better to group discussion, rather than one in which the leader speaks to one member who responds to the leader, and then again the leader speaks to a second member who replies, and so on.

One who acquires skill in leading a discussion is thereby becoming a certain kind of leader:

He is learning to be *patient enough to listen*. This is not easy — for some people. Have you ever known a teacher who could talk fluently but could never stop long enough to listen to what others had to say? Professor Hymes chose a good title for one of his books, *Teacher, Listen, — the Children Speak.* Apply it to this situation. The teacher who is not a good listener will never be a good discussion leader.

He will try to *use every contribution* made in sincerity, even if it does not add greatly to the knowledge of the world. For most pupils need encouragement. If the contribution is most inadequate, one may at least say, " Yes, and would you add. . . . ? "

He will be *as unobtrusive as possible,* keeping as much in the background as he can as long as all is going well, but occasionally coming forward to draw a pupil out, to give a fact, to ask a question, or to summarize what has been said. He will be enough of a teacher to be more concerned about seeing to it that pupils think for themselves rather than " getting the ground covered " or letting the class know just what he thinks about the point at issue.

He will be *on good and easy terms with his pupils* — pleasant, not tense — especially if there are differences of opinion.

He will *not be impatient if members do not take up the discussion readily.* A man was asked to lead a youth group and make it a discussion period. He began by saying, " Our theme for today is so-and-so and this is a discussion period. What do you want to discuss? " There was silence. He repeated his question. " What do you think about it? Or what questions do you have? " Still silence. " Well, then," he said, " we may as well quit," and dismissed the group. The good discussion leader may have to try many approaches, but always with good-humored patience. He may propound a question. If it brings no response, he may give an incident and ask for opinions on what happened. He may restate his question in other words. Of course he will give pupils time to think and to formulate questions or statements in their minds, and not be the kind of leader who says, "Any questions? " Five seconds pause. " Well, if there are none, we'll adjourn." Most of us require a little time to think and to organize what we want to say. We may even need a little prodding, drawing out, or encouragement. This means that the good leader cannot be hurried. If necessary, he may call on one of the group by name for an opinion. But with patience he will get things started.

He will be *sufficiently objective to see both sides of a debatable question,* not thrust his own views upon the class, nor try to suppress differences of opinion. This thought is well expressed in *The Mind Alive:*[2]

. . . the best discussion leader is not the one who becomes nervous whenever deep differences show up and are vigorously pushed. He is not the one who immediately and anxiously sets himself to induce within the group at least the surface appearance of unanimity. He is rather the one who can emotionally tolerate strong disagreements without letting the adversaries so take over the situation that other members are denied their fair say.

Sometimes a leader's unwillingness to have any point of view other than his own brought out may be traced to the fact that he is essentially a propagandist rather than an educator. Sometimes it may be traced to fear on the leader's part; he thinks he will have to answer another point of view and he is not sufficiently sure of himself to do so. But he does not have to answer — all he has to do is to let the views expressed become part of the material for group discussion.

While welcoming an atmosphere of freedom, and indeed encouraging it, he will *not let the reins get out of his hands,* even for a single minute. That is the function of a good leader — to remain in control — which he may well do even though he keeps silent himself for minutes at a time.

He will *know what is discussable and what is not,* for there is no point in attempting to apply the techniques of group discussion to a question on which it is impossible for informed opinion to be divided. We do not have a group discussion on whether the Jordan River flows from the Sea of Galilee to the Dead Sea. It is a fact, and although some may not know the fact, there is no point in considering it *pro* and *con.* There is no point in conducting a guessing game and calling it a discussion. If, however, we take the statement that " gambling, even on the smallest scale, is bad for those who engage in it and for society at large," we have a discussable question on which informed opinion is divided. " Every word of the Bible was verbally inspired ";

[2] Harry and Bonaro Overstreet, *The Mind Alive.* W. W. Norton & Co., 1954. p. 233.

" Christian missions deserves our support "; " The only safe and right position in regard to alcoholic beverages is total abstinence"; " Jesus' teachings in the Sermon on the Mount are practicable and applicable today ";— these are discussable questions, for all represent positions on which informed opinion is divided.

Similarly it is a waste of time to use this method on issues of no importance. In our church school teaching, therefore, we shall lean toward the discussion method when there is room for differences of opinion and when the subject is relevant to our Christian education purposes. We must be able to state clearly the question which is being discussed so that everyone in the group sees it as a problem and understands what the alternatives are. Sometimes we start with a question that soon appears to need refining: " Christian missions deserves our support " may seem at first to be the theme we want to discuss, but it may soon be clear that there are so many different approaches to missions that the Christian missionary effort carried on in some ways warrants support, whereas we are doubtful about the wisdom of supporting it when carried on in certain other ways. We may then modify our question so that it becomes: " Christian missions as carried on by our own denominational board deserves our support." The issue needs to be clear in the mind of every member of the class.

Something of the discussion method or the conversation method may be used in most of our teaching, even when there is no likelihood of conflicting points of view, and when the theme does not suggest a debatable question. The good primary or junior teacher knows this. In a lesson on " The Good Samaritan " or " Joseph Forgiving His Brothers " or " The Bible in English " there may be occasional differences of opinion, even though the theme is not essentially controversial. Still, good teaching calls for skill in using the discussion method. The teacher must not do all the talking. It must be a co-operative enterprise. The lesson can be developed by the conversational method. There must be questions and comments and the exchange of ideas, and the feeling that the group is working together, talking together, thinking together, and deciding together. The teacher who has acquired skill in leading a discussion on debatable questions finds this skill carrying over into all forms of teaching.

A FEW SIMPLE RULES

Any teacher who is trying to acquire skill as a discussion leader may well set for himself a few simple rules:

1. *Let no one monopolize the time.* A comment that we most frequently hear in connection with a discussion group is at this point: " How much better it would have been if A had not tried to do all the talking! " If A is permitted to exercise his propensities for verbal expression there will be no group discussion at all, but something that more nearly approaches a monologue — or perhaps a dialogue between A and the leader. A may enjoy it thoroughly, but not the other members, and it is important to keep the entire constituency in mind. Few will deny the validity of this point but it is not always easy for a leader to put the principle into practice.

Still, he must try. If he is learning to keep the reins in his hands throughout, he will find it increasingly easy to deal with the one who tends to monopolize the time. Incidentally this time-monopolizer may be a primary child; he may be a high school student; he may be an adult; but unless he is restrained there will be no satisfactory group discussion.

The time-monopolizer may not hesitate to break in when another is speaking. But the leader must be adamant in holding to the rule of " one at a time." The time-monopolizer may have the answer to every question that is raised. But the leader must be firm in saying: " This time we want to hear from one who has not yet taken part in the discussion." The time-monopolizer may tend to take three times as long as necessary whenever he makes his contribution. But when he pauses for breath, the leader must be ready to break in and politely steer the conversation in another direction or toward another person. The group itself may make its own rules if any such procedure seems necessary, as is often done in parliamentary bodies, so that there is a limit to the number of times one may speak, or so that each one has a time limit, which in a church school class should be short. Since we are dealing with group thinking and group action it is the group that has a right to decide these things, but the leader is the person responsible for keeping things moving well. With all the tact at his command, the teacher must be firm in seeing that no one member takes an inordinate proportion of the time.

2. *Draw out the more silent and retiring members of the group.* This cannot be left to chance. It is not enough to say that George is not inclined to say much in class and let it go at that. George must be encouraged to participate, for that is a part of his Christian training. He needs individual attention and personal concern at this point, just as everyone needs something of the individual approach in all our teaching efforts.

The most silent is not necessarily the least capable. Temperament has much to do with it, and it may be that the most vocal is the least thoughtful and the one whose knowledge is most limited. When this is true, the group ought to profit by what this more silent member could contribute; the more silent member, moreover, needs the growth which will come from greater participation.

There is nothing inconsistent with free group discussion for a leader sometimes to call on one by name, asking his opinion on this or that, or asking for a bit of information that he may have, bearing on the theme of the day. The more timid the member, the more simple the question needs to be, and if a teacher knows a pupil's real ability he may draw him out to make a contribution far more significant than any that the more loquacious have been making. For him to be brought across the barrier of reticence is part of his training. Just as an adolescent sometimes finds it physically impossible to take the initiative in expressing himself in a group, but — once the first impossible barrier has been hurdled — finds it a little easier from that point on; so the more silent in the group may gradually become a normally participating member, if he can be helped across the first hurdle. But the wise leader will begin in a way that is easy for the retiring type and not be insistent in his requests. A special request for a brief report on some matter important in the discussion may be the start this one needs. Certainly the leader's aim must be to bring every member of the class into some participation in group discussion.

3. *Keep on the track.* The human mind is like a railway network, with switches and spurs and branch lines. Starting on the main line, the train is sent off in another direction by an open switch. It is the same way in group discussion. One person's comment opens up a new line of thought and another continues on that course. He uses an illustration. A third member picks up the illustration, forgetting the point it was meant to illustrate. This reminds the fourth and fifth of something else, and the discussion has departed completely from the supposed point of interest.

It is like this: a class is making a study of Christianity in India and the specific point of the day's discussion is this: " Has the progress of the church in the villages of India been such as to justify the efforts of Christian missions? " It has been made clear that in thousands of these villages there is a Christian community, even though small in comparison with the total population. Someone comments, " But I read in a book the other day that an Indian Christian himself, in government service, had severely criticized his fellow-churchmen because, as he said, they seemed to have lost their early fervor and were not as ardently evangelistic as they ought to be." " Talking about government service," said another, " I have just read an article on an interview with Nehru, in which Nehru was quoted as saying, ' Why didn't the United States recognize Red China? ' " A third was vehement against recognizing Red China and added that there were altogether too many communists in the United States. A fourth found it difficult to make up his mind whether the congressional investigating committees helped the situation or made it worse. From that point they held for some time to one point, but it was far removed from the question the group was supposed to be discussing!

The trouble was in the leadership. Freedom of approach in group thinking should not deteriorate into chaos. Although there are times when we derive great value from the unrestrained freedom of conversation, whether of a company of friends in the living room or of a gathering that follows the techniques of Group Dynamics, organized group discussion needs to hold to the point. And it is the leader's place to see that it does.

In his effort to avoid monopolizing the conversation, and thus to change discussion into a lecture, the leader must not go to the other extreme and let the members run in all directions at once. He is a referee — or better still, a steersman. It is his function to keep the members from wandering and going off on tangents. He keeps in mind constantly what the question for discussion is. If one veers off, this leader may say, "That is an interesting observation, but let's get back to the point at issue." He may repeat it occasionally. He may suggest a question now and then. While he is holding back the one who is inclined to monopolize and encouraging the more timid, he is also keeping both of them — and the rank and file whose temperament lies between — on the track.

This applies even to young children of the primary age. The teacher of children knows this from experience, and anyone who reads the word-for-word reports of class sessions finds examples to substantiate it. If we are to have good teaching, the principle of freedom must not be carried to the point of complete, unrestrained freedom. In a conversation period, children will say many things that bear on the subject, but it is equally true that a child here and a child there will introduce irrelevant comments and make outlandish statements in order to be funny and to provoke a laugh from the class. The good teacher recognizes a child's motives, and knows when this is the case. The good teacher knows how much of this irrelevancy to allow, and when it is time to check it. There is no reason to permit class conversation to run entirely afield of the day's thought, for even a primary class can be kept reasonably well on the track. To do this, a teacher may raise a pointed question that will unconsciously bring the class back to the theme of the day. One of the many values of such a procedure is that it helps to train a child in the ability to concentrate upon one subject at a time. It is a mistake to suppose that children's comments must never be disregarded, and never guided into new directions, or that everything children say is significant. Starting with a story or question, the good teacher does not permit conversation to ramble on aimlessly. There is danger today of over-emphasis upon the significance of analyzing a child's personality through his every rambling remark, and thus losing the values that come from keeping attention focused upon the theme of the session. It is not only the leaders of young people and adults who need to learn how to keep a discussion on the subject; it is also the teachers of children, in their conversation periods, who need to acquire something of the same art.

4. *Have both sides of a question presented, and help the group to weigh the arguments on both sides.* This is not easy, for the judicial mind is all too uncommon. Too few of us are ready to see a point of view other than our own, so busy are we fortifying ourselves in our own prejudices. But two of the objects of group discussion are (a) to bring members to an understanding and appreciation (not necessarily an acceptance) of a viewpoint other than their own; and (b) to help people, young or old, to weigh evidence and to make choices.

Occasionally one meets a teacher who has sufficient objectivity to present one side of a mooted question, and then the other side, so that his students are unable to tell which represents the teacher's own views. Sometimes a discussion leader has sufficient skill to draw out from the group, without undue emotion, a defense of one position, and then reasons for the opposite position. Because he has enough of the judicial type of mind to want to know both sides of a question, he is able to help his students, also, toward that much-desired goal.

Young people may be discussing the question: " Is a Christian justified in the moderate use of liquor? " or, in a different realm, " Can prayer really accomplish results? " In both instances, there are points that can be made on both sides. Having come to see both sides, a young person's arrival at his own point of view will be more significant. A junior high group may discuss: " Is gambling wrong?" or "Why should a young person of our age be a member of the church?" In neither case do they want a categorical answer from the teacher. They want to have a part in the discussion, do some of the thinking themselves, see both sides of the question, and in these ways arrive at their own decision. The reason we want this group to have a Christian teacher is not that this teacher knows all the answers, but that he may strive to keep the discussion in the light of Christian teaching. A junior group is deciding on the cause for which its money is to be used; or it may be considering why there should have been a new translation of the Bible. The boys and girls are led to see different possibilities under a teacher who does not tell them how they are to vote or what they are to think, but who leads them into an appreciation of different possibilities and different answers and guides them toward their own decision. A primary class, in a simpler way, has its conversations and talks things over. The children, for example, discuss the way in which they will leave their room after they have been building a scene on the sandtable to represent a Bible story. If they do not clean up, who will? Is it fair to others to leave the room in disorder? They, too, see two sides to the question and decide on a class policy.

There are subjects that have in them more dynamite than others. And there are people who get emotionally upset over viewpoints expressed in discussion that are different from their own. Some are upset over theological questions, some over matters of behavior, some over social issues. How does the wise leader meet these emotional outbursts from members of the group? A certain Group Discussion Clinic worked out its four-point answer:

How Can We Make Constructive Use of Emotional Outbursts? [3]
1. Momentary silence — the "Quaker Method" — and then move on.
2. Avoid reacting to emotion with emotion.
3. When the "emoting person" pauses, she may be asked to repeat her remarks for clarification. This may help her to see that her manner of speaking has not been very effective in conveying her views.

[3] From "Consultation, Please," reprinted from *Adult Leadership*, monthly publication of the Adult Education Association of the U. S. A.

4. If feelings are deeply involved it may be well to suggest that consideration of the issue be postponed — to a definite time.

There are times when a church school teacher may profit by such advice. An emotional outburst may be regarded as a presentation of one side. The leader may say quietly, " Now let us see what may be said on the other side."

5. *Try to reach a group conclusion.* Every group discussion needs to be brought to a head. It must not be left at loose ends. When there has been considerable talking, with varying points of view, it is possible that the members of the class may leave in some mental confusion. It is the leader who is responsible for preventing this.

The leader may summarize the discussion by reminding the class of the major views that have been expressed and indicating what seems to be the majority opinion. If there has been a vocal minority opinion, that also may be included in the summary.

It may be possible to go further than this, however, and to have not merely the leader's summary but a clearly defined group opinion, with or without a minority view, which the class will accept as its own findings on the subject under discussion. An adult class discussing the subject, " What constitutes a Christian home? " may conclude its discussion with certain points that the members accept as most desirable, if our homes are to be more Christian. A youth group studying "a present-day Christian's creed " may end with a creedal statement of its own — not what the historic creeds say, but, in understandable language, what the members of this class really think about the major questions of the Christian faith, with minority opinions if any so desire. A children's group making a study of the church may have one lesson on " what the church does for boys and girls." Even at this age and on this theme, with less likelihood of the controversial than in older groups, it helps to write the children's contributions on the blackboard and to mark the points on which they agree, so that the simple discussion may be brought to a logical conclusion.

The leader who is conducting a discussion, whether on a controversial subject or not, whether with mature participants or with those who are immature, does well to allow sufficient time at the end for summary and for a clear statement of the conclusions of the class. This gives a feeling of completion which is so often absent from such an experience. Every member should feel that something has been achieved in this class period or in this group of lessons — a feeling that is unlikely if the discussion peters out or stops just anywhere along the way. If the decision is one that looks toward specific action — such as engaging in a service enterprise, giving to a cause, or doing something for the community — this is the time to provide for implementing the decision.

Learning to be a good discussion leader is a long, slow process. The best ones are still learning. To develop satisfactory techniques takes long practice.

This is a skill needed by the teacher of every age. If one is leading a group of parents and teachers on the subject, " Shall the church school give awards? " the easiest procedure would be to make a speech and say what ought or ought not to be done, but a discussion that draws out and evaluates conflicting viewpoints is of more value. If young people are facing the question, " What are we to think of Jesus? " a statement by a speaker is not sufficient, without the opportunity to hear varying points of view and the chance to challenge and to weigh the views of others. Even the simplest conversations with kindergarten and primary children call for expression on their part and questions that stimulate their own thinking, so that the teacher, instead of doing all the talking, guides conversation and brings it to a conclusion. Whether dealing with little children, or youth, or the more mature, the object of the good discussion leader is to inspire pupils to think for themselves.

To lead a discussion requires discipline on the leader's part. The ability to lead a discussion is a skill which all of us as teachers need to acquire and in which we need to grow. Such growth comes through controlled experience.

V

Skills in the Field of Activities

B ETTER TEACHING calls for growing skills also in the field of activities. Teachers are prone to think too much of " next Sunday's session " and not enough of the sessions of a year or ten years hence. It is important that teachers gain skills that will stand them in good stead through the years of the future. The week by week experience of teaching may help to develop activity skills, if one actually makes use of activities; but it is possible for one to continue in the old grooves of talking and telling, and even having group discussion, without ever engaging pupils in activities that have educational value, which they help to determine, and in which they participate. To this end the teaching experience needs to be supplemented by reading and study, by workshops and classes in community training schools, by enrollment in summer laboratory schools and Christian education conferences that will help to develop skills in this field on the part of teachers themselves.

The word " activities " is used in a broad sense. Under it we are including *fellowship activities* that broaden our understanding, give new appreciations, and develop attitudes of friendship and goodwill; *service activities* that express our Christian concern for others; *dramatic activities* that enable our pupils to relive the experiences of others; *creative writing* and expression; and *creative activities in which children use their hands* as well as their minds and words, to increase knowledge, develop new interests, and further the learning process.

In all of these areas the teacher needs as much skill as possible, and such skills can be learned. Some of these activity skills will be used in the classroom; others may be used in out-of-class periods; but all will have value in achieving the aims that prompt us — or that ought to prompt us — to become church school teachers. The important point is not that we acknowledge the significance of these types of activity, but that as teachers we develop sufficient skill to make use of them ourselves, so that we may be able, in turn, to guide our pupils in using them.

FELLOWSHIP ACTIVITIES

Some of the pupil's most significant learning opportunities are apart from the lesson period of the school. There may be fellowship activities which broaden appreciation and experience. These grow out of experiences quite removed from the class hour, even though they are part of the total church school program. If they are a part of the program, then clearly they are planned. However large a place the pupils may have in the planning, there is sure to be an adult adviser. And the better this adult leader succeeds in staying in the background, the greater may be his skill. This is true of fellowship activities which mean so much in Christian growth.

A high school youth group has its International Week End as one of the high points of the year. The members invite young people of other nationalities and races, studying at nearby colleges and universities, to be their guests for most of Saturday and Sunday. The fact that guests are a few years older than their hosts seems to make little difference. On Saturday afternoon these guests come to the church in the suburban community, sixty to seventy-five in number. The hosts take the guests to their homes, one or two or three to a home. All return to the church for their "international banquet" with its welcomes and responses, followed by square dancing or some other program of fun. The visitors spend the night and have breakfast at the homes of their hosts. On Sunday morning all are together at the youth program of the church, and then at the church worship service. Dinner is in the various homes, and in the afternoon all are in the church again for a farewell tea, at which the youth group is supplemented by many adults of the church. Aside from the values that such an enterprise has for the visitors, the whole experience is meaningful for the members of the youth group. It gives them new friend-ships across racial and national lines; it deepens their appreciation of other cultures and helps them to understand the oneness of the human family; it is as much a part of their Christian education as are the things they do by themselves on Sunday morning. But to carry out the week-end so successfully, the skilled leadership of men and women has been required — adults with skill in making the proper contacts, in organizing a big project, in working with the young people to see that interesting activities are planned, in being true hosts, or — if you prefer — in being guides to those who are called hosts. It is this kind of skill that is an asset to a church school teacher.

Some junior high boys and girls went from their church school to a junior high summer camp. For many reasons, some indefin-able, the week was one never to be forgotten; but one of the reasons was the presence on the leadership staff of a Jewish rabbi of unusual charm and ability. Not only did the boys and girls learn much about Jewish customs and festivals, but they came to appreciate this man of another cultural group. It did some-thing for them. It changed their attitudes and broadened their circle of friendship — not by the inclusion of just one more per-son, but by the inclusion of another cultural group. It took skill to bring this about — skill on the part of those who planned the camp and skill on the part of the local church leaders who knew how to steer the young people toward such a summer experience.

A vacation church school with its pupils ranging in age from five to eleven had an outing — not by themselves — but with children of other vacation church schools nearby, white and Negro, American and foreign. Their course of study during these weeks had been on " Boys and Girls Around the World " and this had prepared them, unconsciously, for such an intergroup ex-perience. It took skill on the part of the leaders to bring the children together on the basis of genuine friendship, without any attitude of superiority or condescension, to play with them as comrades, rather than as if they were " doing something for the others."

Fellowship activities beyond one's own church walls belong in the program of Christian education; and that teacher is fortunate who knows how to direct his pupils toward participation in such a program.

The leader must be the right kind of person himself — one who is a world-Christian at heart, believing that " God's children live in many lands " and that human friendship must cross the barriers that man so often raises. This leader must have the ability to treat people as people, not snobbish nor patronizing toward them on the one hand, nor over-solicitous on the other. We sometimes think only of the first of these two attitudes as important. A student worker who tried earnestly to cultivate the attitude of friendliness toward everybody became well acquainted with a Negro student. One day she asked this girl, " Tell me frankly — have you felt that I treat you in just the same way as I do other girls? " The answer surprised her: " No. You sometimes treat me too well. You go out of your way to be nice to me because I'm not a white girl. I wish you could treat me just the same way as you do the others."

The good teacher must be able to plan and to organize. For among the many leadership abilities which the church school teacher needs, skill in inspiring fellowship activities must be included.

SERVICE ACTIVITIES

Not far from the church there was an orphans' home. Fortunately it was not called " The Orphans' Home " but " Cliffdale House." Each Sunday some of the children were brought to this church school and four of them were in the kindergarten. The house mother invited all the children in the kindergarten to a party, and to see the big House. Of course they had a happy time. The next Sunday, in their conversation period, they talked about the party, and before they knew it they were saying how nice it would be to make a present to the House for Christmas, just two weeks off — a picture for a place on the wall that had no picture.

Their birthday money was their " Money for Others," and they decided to use some of it for the purchase of a picture. So the next day their teacher and three of the children went to a store and picked out a picture they liked. The whole kindergarten department took it over to the " House " on the day before Christmas as a Christmas present.

A junior department in its regular course of study had a unit on India. This gave them a good opportunity to find out about the children of India — their home life, how they played, the way they dressed, their schools. They discovered, too, that the number of doctors is fewer, and the medical facilities much less adequate than they enjoyed in their own home town, and that their church with other churches supported a Christian hospital at Vellore. They all wanted to send gifts to the children at this hospital. On a given day they brought crayons, picture books, colored paper, and other articles they thought children of India, sick in a hospital, would like. They packed the box themselves and chose three of their number to take it to the post office and mail it.

The young people of a denominational youth fellowship decided, through their national council (with representatives from all the states), to inaugurate a plan that they called a " Work Day for Christ," when all who were willing to co-operate would spend as much of the day as possible in physical work, the entire receipts to be used for " Our Christian World Mission," their denomination's world-wide program. In one state (like the majority of others) the state youth executive committee approved the idea and invited every church group to co-operate. One church youth group received the request, discussed it at a business meeting, voted heartily to co-operate, and had a day of car washing, when people of the church and neighborhood brought their cars to be washed by a willing and happy group of high school boys and girls. A substantial amount was realized for Christian work at home and abroad. In another church the youth group considered the matter, gladly voted to join others in the project, extended the time from the one Saturday to two days, adding

Friday because it happened to be a school holiday, thanks to a teachers' convention. They raked yards, washed windows, did baby sitting and various other odd jobs, and as a result were able to make a generous gift of almost $200 to " Our Christian World Mission."

In every case, and in quite different ways, the Christian education program was interesting and effective. Teachers may teach and pupils may learn through service activity as well as in the classroom. Such activities are a part of one's education — not merely a result of it, a separate experience. The educational process is not complete until we have done something about our teaching. It is not education " plus " giving money or doing acts of service; money-giving and service activities are a part of one's education — acts and experiences that have value in themselves, and through which one adds to one's learning and becomes a growing person.

In all of this the teacher plays an important role. If service activities are to be carried on effectively, certain skills on the teacher's part are essential.

It is important that *pupils see a reason for what they do* and it is the teacher's function to make sure that they have the right motivation — not so much by telling them as by leading them to discover for themselves.

This calls for *study of facts and actual situations* through stories, and research and group thinking. It takes skill for a teacher so to guide the learning process that there will be genuine motivation for service activities — not a service activity merely decided and announced by the leader.

This means that *the pupils themselves make suggestions and decisions and engage in the activity* (under guidance), even though this takes longer than a more dictatorial procedure would take. There is real art in being a teacher of this kind, but the first step is to recognize the importance of this kind of leadership.

When pupils engage in service activities *it would be tragic if they did so in a patronizing way, with a sense of superiority,* themselves on a pedestal and those helped on a lower plane!

[64]

There need be none of this; but whether there is or not depends largely on the leader's skill in developing a sense of friendship for others and a growing feeling of the world family. In the three illustrations above there was none of this sense of condescension. With the kindergarten group it was a case of the friendship of child for child. With the junior study group, the box might have been sent with a Lady Bountiful attitude, on the one hand, or, on the other hand, with the same neighborliness that one would show in taking a hot dish to a sick neighbor. In the case of the " Work Day for Christ," the youth group need not have had any sense of pity for others, but rather a feeling that their religion was worth sharing. In every such case the way in which the activity is carried on reflects the leader's skill or lack of it.

Service activities furnish a fine chance to develop leadership ability on the part of pupils. They look for service opportunities; they weigh choices; they make decisions; they do things themselves; they manifest good or unfortunate attitudes; they drop a responsibility at the half-way point or carry it through to completion. In this whole procedure there is a chance to increase youthful leadership. But this task of developing youth leadership demands skill in the leader of youth.

Throughout the service enterprise the good teacher keeps in the background as much as possible, calling attention to something here and making a suggestion there, but always letting pupils do what is done and decide what is to be decided, as far as possible. It takes more skill for a teacher to do less, and less skill to make all the decisions and issue all the instructions himself.

INFORMAL DRAMATIZATION

Another effective method of teaching is informal dramatization. It is no new method, for it has been used for many years. It is not widely used, however, because most teachers are timid about attempting it, not quite knowing how to proceed.

If it needs any justification this may be found in the fact that informal dramatization is one of nature's own methods. Watch children at play and you see it in operation. A three-and-a-half-year-old child was on the porch with only an adult. " Will you play ' baby ' with me? " she asked. Of course the adult agreed. At once the three-and-a-half-year-old began: " You be the baby and I'll be the Mommy. Now, Baby, it's time for you to take your nap. Lie down on the porch swing. Are you covered up? . . . Here is a cover to put over you . . . Oh, there's the telephone. (She hurries to the end of the porch) . . . Hello! Hello! Yes. No, Baby can't go out now. She's taking her nap. She can't go out till two o'clock. Good-bye. . . . Did that wake you up, Baby? . . . Well, go to sleep again till two o'clock. . . ." And so it continued.

That was spontaneous, informal dramatization. Why cannot church school teachers build more on this play impulse which is present in everyone? We see it in younger children; but it is in older children as well — and in young people, and in men and women, as shown by the present-day interest in role-playing at parent-teacher gatherings or in other adult groups.

This section has nothing to do with " giving a play," at least not in the sense of selecting something in print and having partici-pants learn parts and work up to a finished production. That is a different kind of experience; valuable though it may be for young people and adults, it is not the kind of dramatics for elementary school children, and is vastly different from what is often called " educational dramatics." When the teacher of children uses the dramatic method as a way of teaching, she does not begin with a written play which will face children with the chore of learning parts. She begins with a story or an experience, real or imaginary, and children " play it " with freedom and spontaneity. A recent writer in *Childhood Education* says something to the effect that when a teacher wants to use the dramatic method with children and turns to a book of plays, it reflects a lack of faith in children, or a lack of faith in one's own ability to bring out the creative in children.[1]

[1] See article by May I. Young, in *Childhood Education,* September, 1954, page 31.

Every good teacher wants to build on interest. Then use informal dramatics occasionally, for it catches children's interest at once; they see it as a form of play. Every child wants to create, to decide, and to build things himself. Then use educational dramatics from time to time, for in it children are making up their own statements, deciding what should be said and done, and what emotion the situation calls for. Every teacher wants to see some results of his teaching in the lives of pupils. Then use the dramatic method, for it makes it easier to understand the subject matter being taught, and the process of dramatization develops self-confidence, the ability to work with others, and other desirable attitudes. It also leads toward deeper religious feeling.

If these things are true it would seem that the method would be more widely used, especially by kindergarten, primary, and junior teachers. There are various reasons why it is not more widely used: sometimes we are so cramped in our equipment that there is not enough room to move about as dramatization requires; or other classes are at our elbows and must not be disturbed; even then, there is sometimes a kitchen, an assembly room, or a neighbor's house to which a class may go for a few weeks. Sometimes a teacher says that she does not have time to teach the lesson and also dramatize one of its incidents — not realizing that the time spent in informal dramatization *is* " teaching the lesson," and a pleasant variation from the usual way of doing so. But probably the major reason why informal dramatization is not more widely used is that the teacher does not know how to go about it, feels insecure in such a situation, and lacks the skill required for this particular technique. The growing teacher, however, who strives to acquire new skills, includes skill in guiding a children's group in informal dramatization.

A pioneer book in this field, published in 1918, summarized twelve steps as a working basis for one who is a beginner in this field and is anxious to develop leadership skill in educational dramatics. More recent writers have not varied greatly from these steps in procedure:

[67]

1. Select a story with care; then adapt it for telling.
2. Tell the story, emphasizing the essential parts.
3. Let the children divide the story into pictures or scenes.
4. Have a discussion of what should take place in each scene.
5. Let volunteers from among the children act out one scene as they think it should be done, using their own words.
6. Develop criticism by the other children with suggestions for improvement.
7. Have a second acting of the scene for improvement.
8. Let each of the other scenes be worked out in the same manner.
9. See that every child has the chance to try out many parts.
10. Play the story through many times. Change it often according to the criticism, until the children recognize the result as a product of their best effort.
11. With the help of the children change the words into biblical form.
12. Let the group assign definite parts for the final performance.[2]

CREATIVE WRITING

Another type of activity that calls for specialized skill on the teacher's part is creative writing. It is being used increasingly in our better church schools, and would be used more if volunteer teachers recognized its value and felt competent to lead their pupils into this kind of experience.

When we advocate creative writing in the church school we are not expecting to see great literature produced. We are expecting, however, that something will be produced that is a sincere expression of genuine feeling on the part of the pupil or of the group — something that has definite value for the pupil or for the class which has engaged in the activity and which, in varying degree, will be appreciated by others also.

The kind of creative writing we have in mind is suitable for almost any age. It may take the form of a prayer, to be judged on the basis of the age and experience of the one or ones whose prayer it is. It may be a story or a description of what one has seen or done. It may be a litany to be used in the school or department. It may be a group letter. It may be poetry with its own particular message and feeling.

[2] Elizabeth Erwin Miller (Elizabeth Miller Lobingier), *The Dramatization of Bible Stories*. Now out of print.

Those who have encouraged children or young people to express themselves in this way testify to the value of so doing. As it is an expression of the best that is in one, leaders find that it results in an appreciation for the best in life. Because what pupils produce may be used in group worship, a new interest in group worship is developed. When a teacher has acquired some skill in leading a class in creative writing, this class, while engaged in such an activity, is unlikely to be troubled by serious disciplinary problems.

How does a teacher approach the task of leadership in creative writing? No doubt in many and various ways, but it may be in such ways as these:

1. *Without ever talking about appreciation one may set the stage for new appreciations of values that seem important.* Carefully chosen articles properly placed around the room will help: a worship center with a flower, or an open Bible, or a cross; a picture or two on the wall to suggest happy home life, or a religious theme suitable for the age; autumn leaves, or a plant, or anything that suggests the beauties of nature. Well-chosen music is another asset, and there is value in pausing at times to think of the words of one of the fine hymns. It will help, also, to introduce children to great pieces of literature such as:

> "Make a joyful noise unto the Lord, all ye lands." (the 100th Psalm)
> "O come, let us sing unto the Lord." (Psalm 95: 1-7a)
> "God be merciful unto us and bless us." (Psalm 67)
> "But where shall wisdom be found." (Job 28: 12-28)
> "Wherewith shall I come before the Lord." (Micah 6: 6-8)

And there are scores of other great pieces of literature, for which a child or youth or adult may cultivate deep feeling.

2. *When a leader has creative writing in mind as a possible activity, let him see that it is properly motivated.* A group may write a litany in order to have it to use in the department worship service. A story or a description of an event may be written to be put in the church paper or the local paper. A prayer may be writ-

ten as the group's own class prayer. A poem may be written for the class record book. Better still, any of these may be done for the sheer joy of it — to express the thoughts and emotions of the members of the group.

3. When engaged in creative writing of a litany or a poem, the class or the individual must have a theme. They must have decided on the subject about which they are to write. The skilled teacher then sets the stage with this theme in mind, and sees to it that there are articles in the room that suggest it, that readings are selected that have a relationship to it, that pupils' mind-set will be toward this theme.

The good teacher will not, as a rule, announce the theme, but in group conversation will draw out the members of the class so that they make the decision. The teacher's skill appears in guiding the thinking, making an occasional suggestion, steering them away from inappropriate trains of thought. Still, the decision may be very different from what the teacher would have predicted. If each individual class member is to write his own, the themes may be the same or different; if it is to be a group enterprise — a single piece of writing — there must be agreement on the theme. The possibilities for themes are legion, for example:

I like my church
Our beautiful world
I'm thankful for my home
My Bible
The person I want to be

The logical place to find a theme is in the course of study. If a class is studying the life of Jesus, you would expect their creative writing of a litany or poem or psalm to be related to Jesus or his teaching. If they are studying the church you would expect their creative writing to have to do with the church. If they are engaged in a world-friendship unit, that should furnish the inspiration for their creative writing. But in every case there are so many possible variations of the basic subject that thought and planning and guidance are needed to arrive at the specific theme within the larger area of study.

4. *If each child or youth is doing his own individual piece of writing the whole class may be at work at the same time.* Sometimes they will be sufficiently interested to want to carry on at home and on the following Sunday bring back what they have done. Of course, they will share their work with one another. The teacher can always find something to appreciate in any sincere piece of work, however crude it may appear. And appreciation comes first. When classmates make their comments, the leader may protect the idea of appreciation by holding them for a time to the question: " What do you like best about it? " Then, if there are suggestions for improvement they will be constructive — not negatively critical.

5. *If the creative writing is a group activity, the teacher may use the blackboard to write down the contributions that the pupils make.* Sometimes they will have an idea and there will be a number of suggestions as to ways of expressing it, before they agree on what is to be written down. At first the blackboard may contain — not a poem nor a litany, but the *makings* of a poem or a litany. The next step is to put it all together as a unit, perhaps omitting some items that have been noted. Then, as a group, they will go over it with care to change a word here or add a word there or smooth out a rough place or improve the rhythm. With young people it sometimes happens that they will divide into four or five groups (similar to the buzz session method), each to write a stanza on a given theme, then all to report back and to consider what they have as a unit.

6. *Make some use of the creative writing that is done by members of the class or by the group itself.* Some of it may be kept permanently in class record books. Some of it may be used to enrich services of worship. Some of it may find a place in the classroom for the year. Children's Day (Church School Day), which ought to reflect the program of the year that is closing, is an excellent time to use some of the creative writing of the year: a litany, a poem, a prayer. If each member of the class is keeping

some kind of notebook on the year's work, it should surely contain the pupil's own creative writing and that of the class as a group. Because this is an activity that catches the interest of pupils themselves, it is easy to make use of whatever creative writing a class does. This interest of the pupils has its effect on other parts of the church school program. One teacher, for example, is quoted as saying that she noticed a growing interest in the Psalms her boys and girls were memorizing because of the fact that they were themselves writing something somewhat similar to the Psalms.

For the benefit of any reader who may have had no experience in creative writing a few examples are given of individual writing and of group writing:

1. *A Poem*

Be thankful, for spring has come.

Our bulbs are blossoming,
    For spring has come.

The robins are coming back from the South,
    For spring has come.

The birds are singing,
    For spring has come.

The boys are talking about baseball,
    For spring has come.

Kites are flying, for spring has come.[3]

2. *On Our Chapel Door* (Lines written to be placed there)

Come quietly
For this is a place of prayer

Sing clearly
For this is a place of praise

Think of Him here
For this is God's House.[4]

[3] Written by a second-grade group, The First Church (Congregational) in Newton Centre, Massachusetts, Mrs. George S. Winsor, Director of Religious Education.
[4] Written by the primary department, The First Church, Newton Centre, Massachusetts.

3. A Christmas Litany

Leader: For the pure white snow,
For trees that glow,
Congregation: Our Father, we thank Thee.

Leader: For the birds and flowers
That give us many happy hours,
Congregation: Our Father, we thank Thee.

Leader: For our friends and neighbors
That do us many favors,
Congregation: Our Father, we thank Thee.

Leader: For the freedom to worship as we like,
For giving us both day and night,
Congregation: Our Father, we thank Thee.

Leader: For sending Jesus to us on earth,
So men might have a new rebirth,
Congregation: Our Father, we thank Thee.[5]

4. An Imaginary Letter About Jesus Blessing the Little Children
(Mark 10: 13-16)

Dear Jane:

The most wonderful thing happened to me today. Jesus was in our village and I saw Him. We gathered flowers because we know Jesus loves them and we all went to see Him. When we got there we could see He looked very busy talking with His followers and one of them told us to go away, Jesus was too busy to be bothered with children. We were so disappointed and unhappy. But Jesus saw us and heard what His helpers said and He stopped talking and turned toward us and held out his arms and said, let the children come to me. And Jane we all ran to him with our flowers and asked Him to tell us a story. And He told us a story and just before we left He put His hand on my head. This is a day I will never forget.

Love,
Mary.[6]

[5] Written by the lower junior department (grades three and four), First Congregational Church, Winchester, Massachusetts, under the leadership of Mrs. Thomas J. Walsh.

[6] Written by a fifth-grade girl in a class taught by Miss Doris Symonds, Old North Congregational Church, Marblehead, Massachusetts.

5. A Statement of Belief

I believe in God as the Creator and loving Father of all men.
I believe in Jesus Christ, his Son, who came to teach men a better
  understanding of God, and to love each other.
I believe as a follower of Jesus
And as a member of the Church
That I must practice what Jesus taught:
  To seek God for guidance
  To treat all men as equals
  To put my church life first
  To be aware of God at all times

In these ways I hope to lead a better Christian Life.[7]

CREATIVE ACTIVITIES IN WHICH CHILDREN USE THEIR HANDS

Among the most important kinds of activity in which the
church school teacher needs to develop skill are those which use
the hands, that broaden the pupils' understanding and appreciation and enlist their interest. Is it necessary to add that this does
not include the old-time " busy work " such as coloring cards and
carrying on various other dictated enterprises? It does include the
handwork that is really creative.

Occasionally one finds a prejudice against such a procedure.
This reminds us of the outcries a century ago against " seculariz-
ing Bible teaching " when leaders had the temerity to make use
of the blackboard as a teaching aid. Dr. Benjamin P. Browne tells
us how church officers looked askance at such doings. It was
daring, a strange innovation, sacrilegious![8] We see vestiges of the
same attitude today when a person finds a children's group painting, or drawing, or modeling with plasticene, or making notebooks, and says, " When do they take up the lesson? They had
better be studying the Bible."

[7] A group statement prepared by a ninth-grade class of The First Church
(Congregational), Newton Centre, Massachusetts, Mrs. George S. Winsor,
Director of Religious Education.

[8] See " Highlights from the Colorful History of the Sunday School Movement " by Benjamin P. Browne in *The International Journal of Religious
Education*, September, 1954.

More often, however, we meet not with prejudice, but with fear. Teachers are afraid to introduce creative handwork because they do not know how to begin. They need skills along this line — skill in knowing how to use their own hands in these ways and skill in guiding the children under their care.

Why do we urge that a reasonable amount of the classroom time be used for creative activities with the hands? For one thing, children like it. Because they like it, it holds their interest; and when their interest is held there is always greater effort on their part, and disciplinary problems fade away. Moreover, we learn by doing. No amount of listening can compensate for activity on the part of the pupil. If a child is merely told what a Palestinian village was like, the impression is vague; but if he builds such a village he will always remember. Even seeing pictures is not enough. Thus this form of activity gives him clear concepts that he would never have had through stories, or mere talking, or even seeing pictures. Whatever discussion and conversation children may have will be more meaningful if they have a background of understanding. Finally, when pupils work as a group in an activity in which all are doing something with their hands, the very experience of working together has in it character-building elements that contribute to their Christian training.

The teacher of a kindergarten, or a primary, or a junior class — yes, or a junior high class — needs to develop a reasonable amount of skill in such areas as these:

Making a notebook
Drawing
Using the sand table
Painting
Using potter's clay or plasticene
Making good letters
Making friezes
Making charts and posters
Map-making
Constructing peep shows, motion pictures, and dioramas

How can this be expected of one who has no special talent in these fields and no professional training in art?

So many have found an answer, that clearly others can do so also. If teachers or prospective teachers will take advantage of the opportunities open to them, they will gain sufficient skills to be able to use this method of teaching. What are these opportunities?

1. *Short courses or workshops* in creative activities are offered at Community Training Schools, at Summer Laboratory Schools, at Summer Schools of Christian Education. Hundreds of men and women have been in these workshops and have gotten the start they needed. Much of their teaching by talking has been transformed into teaching through activities. It has revolutionized their methods and has proved itself to be more than worth the effort.

2. *Books are available as helps.* A teacher of serious purpose may study — not merely scan — one of these books, practicing what is suggested as she studies. Among such available books two in particular may be mentioned: *Activities in Child Education* by Elizabeth M. Lobingier, Pilgrim Press, 1950, and *Here's How and When* by Armilda B. Keiser, Friendship Press, 1952.

3. *Practice is essential.* This the teacher needs to do by herself, so that she will acquire enough skill in these various areas to meet her class with confidence, and to be helpful to pupils when they need help. If she has done this, she will not turn aside from creative manual activities through fear.

Every parent and everyone else who observes small children is aware of the utter abandon with which a child of nursery or kindergarten age approaches this form of self-expression. There are no inhibitions! He draws your picture with readiness and assurance. As the years pass by, his inhibitions increase. The teacher is that child grown to maturity — with inhibitions, because she fears that what she does may not be just right. She needs to develop skills.

This teacher also faces the danger of introducing activities with no freedom nor creativity. Many a course of study, in suggesting what to do, includes activity sheets that are stereotyped and but little more than cards to be colored. But the teacher who has been acquiring skill in this field will be able to lift the level of work and substitute activities with more creativity.

This teacher who is gradually gaining skills along these lines needs to remember that what she is proposing may be newer to herself than to her pupils. In their day-school work these boys and girls probably make notebooks, draw a great deal, use poster paints at easels, make friezes for their rooms, and charts and posters. These are activities and techniques in which they are at home. The skills that they have acquired in the day school — or at least the interests to which they have given expression — should be put to work and utilized on Sunday, since these activities serve the purpose of the church school as well as of the day school. To do this, the problem is to bring the teachers up to the expectation and ability of the pupils themselves.

This is not the place for a detailed discussion of each of these various ways of teaching; but we may make a few passing comments.

When *drawing* is introduced into the church school program, the children should have a clear purpose in mind. Their purpose will be to tell a story or to illustrate something of interest or importance. With this in mind, the child will proceed according to his age — the kindergarten child with utter freedom, the primary child with no thought of perspective or of likeness. And the teacher's encouragement is not toward correctness or likeness, but toward the telling of the story in the child's own way. As the child becomes a little older, he himself begins to think about accuracy and perspective as the adult sees it; then the teacher can satisfy the pupil's desire if he, the teacher, has sufficient skill to do so. The good teacher will have many pictures at hand that make their own suggestions to the child: the kind of house in which people lived in Jesus' day; the characteristic of a camel — the hump; the difference between a palm tree and other trees; the kind of tent Abraham used. One will be a better teacher who gains skill by practicing drawing oneself, trying to simplify forms and to use the fewest possible lines for each figure made. The teacher who is growing in such skills may never be an artist, but can learn enough to be helpful and to feel at home in using drawing in the classroom.

Painting is not very different from drawing. Here, too, there must be a purpose — to tell a story, to illustrate something, or to express oneself. The painting of murals on large sheets of paper at the easel may serve the purpose of teaching religion as well as the purposes of the public school. But the teacher needs to have a little of the technical " know-how " herself, in order to be aware of pupil difficulties and to see new possibilities.

In the matter of *modeling* the leader needs practice to the point of feeling at home in modeling objects for a sand table or a diorama, or telling a story, or visualizing how situations appeared, or what people did. Experience will show that in the church school, with only a weekly session, it is better not to use potter's clay, as the day school often does, but plasticene — which does not harden, and which can be used over and over again.

The creative teacher will inspire an interest in *notebooks* that are the pupils' own, with records of what they have done, drawings they have made, accounts of their own dramatizations, any creative poetry or stories or litany of their own or of their group, accounts of service activities, records of fellowship experiences, statements of belief, and glimpses of the year's work. Such notebooks ought to be neat, artistic, pleasing, worthy of being preserved, with some attention given to color and margins and mounting. The leader who has enough skill along these lines to help pupils to make books of this kind has a real advantage over the ordinary teacher.

The word to be emphasized in all of this is *skills*. The teacher must have some growing skills of his own if pupils are to be guided into a wise use of activities of these various kinds that are creative and meaningful.

VI

Skill in Storytelling

T<small>HE</small> place of the story is entrenched, not only in the heart of every child, but in the heart of the race as well. From olden times, when there were no books to read and families gathered about the campfire to listen to an older one tell stories, down to the present day, when children in the home ask for a story, it has held its place of pre-eminence.

Because the story is popular and because it is an important aid in achieving our aims in Christian education, the teacher needs skill in storytelling. This does not mean that the story is the only way of teaching or even that it is necessarily the most important way. During the last half-century it has been overstressed — at least it has been given a primary place, instead of a place on a par with other methods. To all too many teachers it has been synonymous with " the lesson ": if there is a story, there is a " lesson "; if there has been no story, there has been no teaching of " the lesson! " This is unfortunate. As suggested in previous chapters there are other procedures equally effective; learning may take place through conversation and discussion; it may come through some form of activity. We must help teachers to outgrow the time-honored attitude that if the class hour has had no lesson story there has been no real teaching period. There is value in variety. It is important also that more place be given to pupil activity and learning by doing, and that service and fellowship experiences be given their due emphasis as ways of learning. Recognizing the truth of all this, there still remains a big place for the story in Christian training and a need for greater skill in storytelling.

No one doubts the place of the story with younger children. With older boys and girls it still has its place, but the type of story must be different. But what of young people and men and women? The teacher of these older groups also has an asset if he is able to tell a story well. When a minister introduces a story into his sermon and tells it effectively, even the oldest members of the congregation are impressed and moved. It is an art to be able to organize an illustration in the form of a story, with a good beginning and a good ending.

It is important also for the teacher to use the story technique in other ways. In giving a report or in making an announcement, one may organize what one is to say — the beginning, the order of the points to be made, the conclusion — so that the statement is clear and logical. Thus there is no needless repetition, no " I forgot to say " postscript, no unimportant elements.

Perhaps there is nothing new to be said on the subject of story-telling; so many good books are available! Most of them, published a generation or more ago, and a very few recent publications, enunciate principles as sound today as ever. It would not be possible, however, to consider the work of the church school teacher without reference to this important method.

How may one recognize a good story and what are its characteristics?

Judged by every test, some of our best examples come from the Bible. This is fortunate for the religious educator, for it is to the Bible, first of all, that the church school teacher turns for source material. Let us consider one of the Old Testament stories:

Naaman the Leper

Naaman, commander of the army of the king of Syria, was a great man with his master and in high favor, because by him the Lord had given victory to Syria. He was a mighty man of valor, but he was a leper. Now the Syrians on one of their raids had carried off a little maid from the land of Israel, and she waited on Naaman's wife. She said to her mistress, " Would that my lord were with the prophet who is in Samaria! He would cure him of his leprosy." So Naaman went in and told his lord, " Thus and so spoke the maiden from the land of Israel." And the king of Syria said, " Go now, and I will send a letter to the king of Israel."

So he went, taking with him ten talents of silver, six thousand shekels of gold, and ten festal garments. And he brought the letter to the king of Israel, which read, " When this letter reaches you, know that I have sent to you Naaman, my servant, that you may cure him of his leprosy." And when the king of Israel read the letter, he rent his clothes and said, "Am I God, to kill and to make alive, that this man sends word to me to cure a man of his leprosy? Only consider, and see how he is seeking a quarrel with me."

But when Elisha the man of God heard that the king of Israel had rent his clothes, he sent to the king, saying, " Why have you rent your clothes? Let him come now to me, that he may know that there is a prophet in Israel." So Naaman came with his horses and chariots, and halted at the door of Elisha's house. And Elisha sent a messenger to him, saying, " Go and wash in the Jordan seven times, and your flesh shall be restored, and you shall be clean." But Naaman was angry, and went away, saying, " Behold, I thought that he would surely come out to me, and stand, and call on the name of the Lord his God, and wave his hand over the place, and cure the leper. Are not Abana and Pharpar, the rivers of Damascus, better than all the waters of Israel? Could I not wash in them, and be clean? " So he turned and went away in a rage. But his servants came near and said to him, " My father, if the prophet had commanded you to do some great thing, would you not have done it? How much rather, then, when he says to you, ' Wash and be clean? ' " So he went down and dipped himself seven times in the Jordan, according to word of the man of God; and his flesh was restored like the flesh of a little child, and he was clean.

Then he returned to the man of God, he and all his company, and he came and stood before him; and he said, " Behold, I know that there is no God in all the earth but in Israel.[1]

As we read this dramatic story, a number of points stand out:

1. *Much is crowded into a limited space.* There is no useless repetition, no needless detail.

2. When one of the characters speaks, his words are quoted as *direct discourse.* This makes the story more vivid than if indirect discourse had been used.

3. The incident is a *dramatic* one. The reader sees the problem but is uncertain of its solution until almost the end of the story. Interest is thus sustained to the end.

[1] From the *Revised Standard Version of the Bible.* Copyrighted 1946 and 1952. 2 Kings 5 : 1-15b. It is possible to consider the entire chapter as one story. We have chosen to think of this as two stories, the second being the story of Gehazi.

4. There is *action* throughout — not long descriptions that can never hold the interest, but movement and action.

5. The way in which the story *starts* is quick, brief, specific, and to the point. It sets the stage. (See verse 1.)

6. Then comes a *series of activities* — one happening after another, as the story develops, but still the reader is left in doubt as to the outcome. (See verses 2-13).

7. *The high point* — when Naaman did what Elisha had commanded, dipped seven times in the Jordan and (the reader still uncertain as to the outcome) " his flesh was restored like the flesh of a little child, and he was clean." That is the climax.

8. The *conclusion* of the story is short and satisfying: He returned to Elisha and said: " Behold, I know that there is no God in all the earth but in Israel."

One who is trying to improve his storytelling technique may well keep these points in mind. The first four are important characteristics of the good story: (1) brevity, rather than wordiness; (2) the use of direct discourse; (3) a dramatic plot; and (4) plenty of action.

The last four points are equally important as giving us an analysis of a good story: (1) the way it starts; (2) a series of activities; (3) the high point; and (4) the conclusion.

Take another illustration, this one a New Testament story — Jesus' parable of the Lost Boy, better known as the parable of the Prodigal Son:

There was a man who had two sons; and the younger of them said to his father, " Father, give me the share of property that falls to me." And he divided his living between them. Not many days later, the younger son gathered all he had and took his journey into a far country, and there he squandered his property in loose living. And when he had spent everything, a great famine arose in that country, and he began to be in want. So he went and joined himself to one of the citizens of that country, who sent him into his fields to feed swine. And he would gladly have fed on the pods that the swine ate; and no one gave him anything. But when he came to himself he said, " How many of my father's hired servants have bread enough and to spare, but I perish here with hunger! I will arise and go to my father, and I will say to him, ' Father, I have sinned against heaven and before you; I am no longer worthy to be called your son; treat me as one of your hired servants.' "

And he arose and came to his father. But while he was yet at a great distance, his father saw him and had compassion, and ran and embraced him and kissed him. And the son said to him, " Father, I have sinned against heaven and before you; I am no longer worthy to be called your son." But the father said to his servants, " Bring quickly the best robe, and put it on him; and put a ring on his hand, and shoes on his feet; and bring the fatted calf and kill it, and let us eat and make merry; for this my son was dead, and is alive again; he was lost, and is found." And they began to make merry.[2]

As we analyze this New Testament story, we find that — like the Old Testament story of Naaman — it divides itself easily into four sections: (1) *The beginning*, verses 11 and 12; (2) *a succession of events*, verses 13-21: he takes a journey; he squanders his substance; there is famine and suffering and, near starvation, he feeds swine; his thoughts go back to his home; he determines to return; he decides how he will meet his father; his return reveals the eager and forgiving father and the penitent son; (3) *the climax*, verses 22-24a; (4) *the ending*, verse 24b.

The majority of the leading writers on storytelling have made some such analysis of its elements. Edward P. St. John,[3] in 1910, spoke of *a beginning, a succession of events, the climax,* and *the end.* Esenwein and Stockard,[4] in 1917, made a three-fold division that really included all four: *the beginning of the story, the body of the story (including the climax), the end of the story.* Jeanette Perkins Brown,[5] in 1951, divided the story in this way: *the introduction, the sequence of events, the climax, the ending.*

Those who prepare our church school curriculum materials try to choose stories suitable for the age. When we, as teachers, sub-

---

[2] From the *Revised Standard Version of the Bible.* Copyrighted 1946 and 1952. Luke 15 : 11-24. Like many Bible stories, the entire passage to the end of the chapter may be regarded as one story or as two. We are regarding it as two and thinking of verses 11-24 as a single and complete story.

[3] Edward Porter St. John, *Stories and Story Telling.* The Pilgrim Press, 1910.

[4] J. Berg Esenwein and Marietta Stockard, *Children's Stories and How to Tell Them.* The Home Correspondence School, 1917.

[5] Jeanette Perkins Brown, *The Storyteller in Religious Education.* The Pilgrim Press, 1951.

stitute other story material or select supplementary stories, we, too, must think of this point of suitability for the particular age-group we are teaching. We must make our selection, moreover, on the basis of the purpose the story will fulfill. At a party, when you are telling a story to a group, or at bed-time, when you are telling a story to a child, you may choose any story that is appropriate and geared to the age and experience of the hearers. In the church school class, however, you have a theme for the day and a stated aim for this class session. Like everything else that you do during the session, the story that is chosen must contribute to the main purpose of the lesson for the day.

The younger the children are, the shorter must the story be, the more important is direct discourse, the more necessary it is to use simple language and short sentences, and the more essential that there be action rather than much description. The younger the children are, the more readily will they respond to the repetition of sounds, words, and phrases in a kind of rhythm; and the more important it is that the setting of the story be in the background of their own experience. In the early elementary school years, children's interests begin to widen, due to their school experience, travel, and television; they are ready, therefore, for stories that are a little longer, with a wider setting, with less repetition, and with slightly more description; but action and direct discourse are still words to remember. Older elementary school pupils are interested in people who achieve things and there is therefore more place for stories of people whose accomplishments are worth while — the hero story and the right kind of biographical sketch. Living in a bigger world, they enjoy tales of children of far places in the world. With young people and adults, we can use the story form as a vehicle for conveying a message as to world problems and telling what is happening here and there as we strive toward a Christian order.

The story in the church school class should be of interest to the pupil, but it should also serve a larger purpose. The good story is a basis for knowledge; it leads to new understanding and new appreciations. It may have an emotional value and lead to the mood of worship. It may pose a problem and bring a solution to the problem, or present alternatives that become a basis for further thought and conversation. The story may reveal attitudes and elements of character that hearers will want to cultivate. It may suggest (although the storyteller may not do the suggesting) new experiences and activities in which the class may engage.

Where does the teacher find good stories to tell? The most obvious place is in the course of study. There may be a story in the pupil's book; in the leader's guide a story may be found that does not appear in the pupil's book. These are appropriate to the subject of the day; having decided which story to use, the teacher then needs to work at the task of telling it effectively. The good teacher, however, goes beyond the lesson books. There are some who keep loose-leaf notebooks of stories that appeal to them, built up gradually through the years. One source is a Christian education magazine; as an example, *Children's Religion* [6] devotes some pages in each issue to new stories for different age groups. If you read ten, there may be two or three that appeal to you, which you may copy in your loose-leaf notebook, or cut out of the magazine and paste in, or merely refer to in a notation, if you keep a permanent file of the magazine itself. The reading books of the interdenominational mission study publications of each year, home and foreign, are an excellent source for stories for different ages. There are many published books of stories, some of which ought to be in the church school workers' library for reference.

It need hardly be said that the Bible itself is the source of our best stories for teaching religion. Probably most of us make too little use of additional Bible stories in church school teaching. A few years ago one of the outstanding preachers of America made a habit of including a children's story in his morning service, and always making it a Bible story, which he told vividly and dramatically. The teacher who keeps a story notebook may well include in it notations of Bible stories by subjects.

Even a person who is fairly familiar with the Bible is likely to be

[6] Published by the Pilgrim Press, 14 Beacon Street, Boston, Mass.

struck by the excellence of its stories — just as good stories — when he reads sections of it with only this point in mind. Try the experiment on the Joseph stories in Genesis. The one on Joseph being sold by his brothers (Genesis 37: 12-35) is an example. Note its short and clear-cut *beginning* (verses 12-14). Then comes the *succession of events* (verses 15-32): he meets a man in the field; he is sent to Dothan; his brothers see him and conspire against him; he is thrown into a pit; he is sold to Ishmaelite traders; Reuben grieves and is afraid; the brothers practice deception — dipping the robe into goat's blood; they report to their father. Then comes the *climax* (verse 33): Jacob is convinced that Joseph has been killed by wild beasts! The *ending* follows (verses 34-35). Throughout, there is action and movement; the story is dramatic; the writer uses direct discourse. The other Joseph stories are worthy of study also, even if merely from the standpoint of a good story.

Read the various stories in Daniel from the standpoint of structure. Take the story, for example, of the deliverance from the fiery furnace (Daniel 3: 1-30). Whether it is to be interpreted as fact or as folk-lore, one cannot help being impressed by its vividness, its movement, its direct discourse, the dramatic element from beginning to end. It, too, follows the same general pattern of a good story: the *beginning* is brief (verse 1); then comes the *succession of events* (verses 2-25): the picture of the great assembly, the herald's command that all fall down and worship at the sound of the instruments, the people's obedience, the accusation to Nebuchadnezzar that three Jews did not obey, their refusal to comply, the act of binding and casting them into the fiery furnace, the appearance of four men — not three — in the fiery furnace, the three men called forth, unhurt; the *climax* is clear (verses 26-29); the *conclusion* is brief (verse 30).

Study the parables of Jesus as examples of good stories; or scores of other parts of the Bible, both Old and New Testaments.

The more capable teacher, moreover, may be able, occasionally, to write his own stories, getting ideas from observation and experience. One who attempts this will want to follow the general pattern that has stood the test of time: a short beginning, a series of activities, a climax, a brief conclusion. When he has written it he may test his story on the basis of such points as this chapter is emphasizing: action; direct discourse; some dramatic incident; no wordiness; no moralizing at the end. Whether or not one attempts to write stories oneself, there is value in having one's own collection of stories which represent many themes that will be useful in church school teaching.

This brings us specifically to the subject of this chapter centering in the word " skill." How may we improve our skill in storytelling?

1. *Telling vs. reading a story.* There is a place for reading stories to a class, as to any other group, or to a single child. But if you read a story to a class, it is important that everything be just right. If you read from a book, the impression is more favorable than if you read from a " quarterly "; it seems more like a real story. It is important, also, that it be read well, without having the eyes glued to the page every moment. There is also such a thing as a favorable way of having the class seated. In crowded quarters it may be necessary for the class to stay around the work table while the story is being read, but this is not ideal. A work table is intended for work; when there is no work going on, it is unfortunate to have boys and girls sprawling all over the table. How much better to have the group gathered about you — whether they are seated in chairs or informally on the floor — you being the focus of attention and the class being comfortably arranged as for conversation or group listening.

Ordinarily in the church school class, however, *telling* a story is much to be preferred to reading it. There is a spontaneity about telling that gives it a real advantage. The storyteller can look the members of the class in the eye, without being bound by the printed page. Every story can be made more meaningful by the personality of the teller, and human personality appears to best advantage through the story that is told, not read. The good storyteller holds the audience to a degree impossible with the story reader. There is nothing between the teller and his hearers.

He can look them in the face, and that makes them look him in the face and holds their attention.

No teacher ought to say: " I can't tell a story. I have to read it." When one is beginning one may not be able to tell a story well; the skill must be learned. Just as we develop skill in golf, or in bowling, or in flower arrangement, or in leading a discussion — by work and practice — so it is in the ability to tell a story.

2. *Bringing the hearers to the point of readiness for the story.* Whether it is a children's group or an adult group, the storyteller should never begin until everyone is ready. This presupposes being comfortable, whether seated in chairs or on the floor, with no light shining in anyone's eyes, in a warm but ventilated room, with no one in anyone else's way, with everyone able to see the face of the leader. It includes being expectant and ready to hear the story. An inexperienced storyteller is in danger of making the mistake of beginning before all eyes are upon him with an attitude of expectancy. Sometimes a quiet "Are we ready? " is enough to bring the group to this point. Children will usually be at the point of readiness if the teacher is at the point of readiness — prepared as far as the story itself is concerned, at ease and natural in manner, talking in a conversational way rather than tending toward the over-dramatic, speaking so that all can hear, adapting his voice to what he is saying, so that he hurries a bit when the action is swift, goes more slowly when the action is retarded and pauses occasionally when a pause is needed for impressiveness, always looking from one to another into the eyes of the hearers.

3. *Outlining the story.* This is important. The inexperienced leader who wonders whether he can possibly do anything but read the story may have his outline in his hands to refer to occasionally. This is a bridge between reading and telling without notes. In making an outline it is well to keep in mind the four divisions or elements in the good story already discussed. This suggests the framework of one's outline.

The *beginning* introduces the story and sets the stage. It is most effective when it is kept brief. I remember an excellent manuscript, a story for boys and girls, which was almost ruined by the first six pages; but when the author decided to eliminate these pages and plunge right into his story, *in medias res*, it became an excellent storybook. Consider Jesus' immortal story of the Good Samaritan. The beginning (Luke 10: 30) sets the stage: "A certain man was going down from Jerusalem to Jericho; and he fell among robbers, who both stripped him and beat him and departed, leaving him half dead." That is short, definite, vivid. In the story, "The Second Mile," by Truman B. Douglass [7] the beginning simply gives a glimpse of the great road, the many travelers, and a boy David watching everything eagerly.

The second division is the *series of activities*, the succession of events. This is the largest part of most stories and may be the longest part of the outline. In the story of the Good Samaritan there are three major events — the priest passing by, the Levite passing by, the coming of the Samaritan. In connection with the third event, there are five separate and important items to be noted in order in the outline. In the story, "The Second Mile," the succession of events that the storyteller might list on his outline are these: (1) David longs to travel; (2) he sees a Roman soldier; (3) the soldier calls him to carry his pack; (4) David's thoughts of hatred; (5) David's thoughts of the Master on this road and of his teaching on the second mile; (6) at the end of the first mile, David's offer and the soldier's surprise; (7) the second mile: they walk together and talk of the Master and of the second mile.

The third element has to do with the *one high point* of the story. It is a single experience — a logical climax to the succession of events. In the story of the Good Samaritan it is found in verse 35 — the Samaritan's declared purpose to do everything needed. In the story, "The Second Mile," it is the parting at the top of the hill: "Good-bye . . . Friend."

The fourth division is the *conclusion*. In the Good Samaritan story it is the question and the answer found in verses 36 and 37,

[7] Reprinted in *The Storyteller in Religious Education* by Jeanette Perkins Brown, Pilgrim Press, 1951, pp. 122-124.

which is in no sense moralizing at the end, but something that is required in view of the fact that the whole story was in answer to the lawyer's question of verse 29. The conclusion must be brief as in this case. Sometimes the ending is simply the " they lived happily ever after " part. Sometimes it just rounds out the story, as in " The Second Mile " — a short ending on David's thoughts: " the Master's words! It works . . . I walked one mile behind an enemy — I walked the second mile and found a friend! "

The outline is an aid — a reminder. It helps one prepare for the telling of a story. At first one may use it, but as time goes on, one feels less and less need of the written outline in the class session.

4. *What about trying to memorize a story?* With most of us, it is dangerous, because if we forget the exact words we become confused. It is much better to memorize ideas or topics, rather than the words of a story. On this basis, if a story is told on three occasions there may be as many variations in words, but the points are the same and the development is the same. Unconsciously one falls into much the same wording at important points in the story, but this is different from memorization, which makes one feel that one must use just the words of the text. If one is to memorize anything, it may be the beginning and the conclusion, allowing for more freedom as one proceeds with the succession of events. The memorized story sounds more stilted; it is better to have it sound as if one is talking freely and conversationally.

5. *The use of direct discourse.* By all means use direct discourse when telling what one of the characters has said. The Bible does this constantly. Experienced storytellers do it. In the story of David and his mighty men he said: " Oh that one would give me water to drink of the well of Bethlehem which is by the gate." At the risk of their lives they brought him the water for which he longed. But he could not drink it! He said: " Be it far from me, O Jehovah, that I should do this; shall I drink the blood of the men that went in jeopardy of their lives? " (See 2 Samuel 23: 13-17.) How much more forceful than if the account had read: " David let the people know that he would like

a drink of water from the well by the gate at Bethlehem. But when the mighty men had brought it, he said that he could not drink it because they had risked their lives in getting it."

In the old folk tale of the sheep and the pig, someone might say that the sheep and the curly-tailed pig said that they would build a house for themselves and live in it together. The storytellers are more effective; they say: "'We will build us a house,' said the sheep and the curly-tailed pig, 'and there we will live together.'"

One person tells Matthew's Christmas story by saying: "The wise men came from the east to Jerusalem and asked where the child was who was born King of the Jews. They said they had seen his star in the east and had come to worship him." The Bible is more vivid; it says: "Wise men from the east came to Jerusalem saying, 'Where is he that is born King of the Jews? For we saw his star in the east and are come to worship him.'"

6. *Reliving the story.* If you do not like a story, do not tell it, for your attitude toward it will have its effect and you will not be able to throw yourself into it with enthusiasm. If it is a story about Albert Schweitzer, you will tell it better if you know something about him and admire him. If you know nothing of him to begin with, you will tell your story better if you get something of a background of his work and his service to humanity through the years. If you are telling a Bible story, read more than the actual verses so that you will know it in its context; it is here that a commentary, a Bible dictionary, and an historical geography will help.

Anna Buckland is quoted as saying that the reason some people cannot tell stories is because they have no story to tell. If your story is about St. Francis of Assisi, or Frank Laubach, or Kagawa, or Grenfell and you know more about the person than is given in this one story, you will have a story to tell. You will know more than you tell and this extra knowledge will enrich what you do tell. For you will know your characters, understand their emotions, and feel the force of the story yourself.

Informal dramatizing gives participants a deeper feeling for a story and helps the teller to tell the story well. It gives a deeper feeling for the action and enables those who participate in the dramatization to enter into its experiences better. Dramatization helps us to appreciate the emotional reactions of the characters. Therefore pupils who have dramatized a story are more ready to have it told again; and the leader who has dramatized it with boys and girls — or by herself in an imaginary way — can more easily relive the story and thus tell it better.

7. *When to end a story.* The time to end a story is when you have reached the end. Having reached the end, don't go on and talk about what you have said. Don't go on and talk about what the story means, or how the hearers should apply it to themselves. Ministers who give children's story-sermons err at this point more than at any other; frequently, having finished the story, they continue: " Now boys and girls, this means. . . ." And the spell of a good story is broken. This applies equally to the church school teacher. The story must carry its own meaning and its own message; if it does, it is unnecessary for the teller to call the listeners' attention to what the meaning and the message may be. The art of storytelling is to allow the story to stand alone and to speak for itself; if it cannot speak for itself, it is not a good story. The cure for a poor story is not to tack something on at the end that is deduced from the story itself, but to substitute a good story.

8. *Continued practice.* Skill in storytelling comes through practice and through work — like playing the piano, learning to draw, or improving your tennis game. If you seek to develop this skill you may pass through various stages: reading a story, reading it better, telling it in your own words with the help of notes, using fewer notes, using no notes, improving your technique through practice. This is an important skill in Christian teaching, recognized chiefly as a need for the teacher of children, but also a valuable tool for the leader of youth, and an asset even to the one who teaches or speaks to adults.

VII

How to Teach Children

How to teach depends upon whom we teach. We teach persons, and persons differ tremendously from age to age. We do not improve our teaching " in general " as much as we improve it specifically — for the nursery age, or for juniors, or for a high school class.

Occasionally we find a person who seems to have the faculty of teaching effectively at many age levels — a capable kindergarten teacher, and also a skillful teacher of junior highs. This is the exception. By training and experience we come to the point where we teach fairly well at one age level, or perhaps two, and it seems only sensible to utilize this experience and training by continuing with approximately the same age group and thus becoming even more proficient in our teaching.

NURSERY CHILDREN

In most church schools this means the three-year-olds. Occasionally the program is expanded to include two-year-olds, or even one-year-olds, but as a rule the nursery class is made up of children who are three, sometimes extended to those who are a few months younger and occasionally continuing a little beyond the age of four.

An erroneous idea persists in the minds of some people that anyone will do to teach in the nursery department, because the pupils are so young and inexperienced. Perhaps this idea is rooted in the misconception of teaching as imparting knowledge or subject matter; from this viewpoint the one who is least capable of assimilating a great amount of subject matter does not require expert teaching. On the contrary, it is probably more difficult to be a good teacher of three-year-olds than of high school students, although I expect no high school teacher to agree! While the average person thinks of the nursery teacher as a kind of babysitter, she is really the one who is giving children their start in Christian nurture — a very different matter. Experience and skill are needed because the task is so delicate and difficult, calling for insights and understandings that many a parent does not possess, and often requiring suggestions to parents. For this reason it is not the place for high school girls unless they are helping as learning assistants.

One reason why the nursery teacher must be chosen with the greatest care is that this is a period of adjustment for the small child. From the environment of the home to the environment of the church school is a great change, calling for expert leadership. Another reason is that the little child is such an individualist that a strong leader is required to guide him as he moves from extreme individualism to even a little socialization. Still a third reason why we need capable persons as teachers of the nursery group is that what is done does not look to a teacher of older boys and girls like a class at all; and yet its significance is just as great as that of the older group's program.

Nursery children gather in the church school, but hardly as a class — as most of us think of a class. The children are doing things by themselves as individuals or in small groups. There is no sense of unity, such as one would find in a fifth-grade class. There is no clearly defined lesson period, plus a worship period, plus a period of group activities. It may be that throughout the entire session there is no time when all the nursery children are together in a group. You will not — or should not — find them all seated around tables, as you might find a class of second graders. The air of informality prevails. The good nursery class or department does not look like a class at all.

The nursery teacher's problem is increased by the fact that it is difficult to define today's " lesson " with the definiteness that a sixth grade teacher would have. Certainly the lesson is not a body of biblical material, nor is it a theme such as a junior high teacher would have. " The lesson " is everything that happens during the session. Instead of thinking in terms of subject matter to be taught in the nursery class, we think of the experiences of the children through which learning takes place. Therefore the teacher's task is to guide experience so that the desired kinds of learning may result.

The most important word to remember is *play*. The visitor usually sees only one thing in the nursery room: the children are just playing! This is another reason why the unthinking say that anyone can teach in this department, for cannot anyone watch a child at play? A writer on this age says that nursery children do just three things: they arrive; they go to work, that is, play; they go home.

How would you describe the play of the nursery child? It is *individual*. They do not play group games, but are happy by themselves. It is *imitative*. As you watch the nursery child you can see in what he does a reflection of his parents, his home life, the activities of his own little world. It is *imaginative*. Who else could build up the fanciful ideas that prompt his activities? It is *dramatic*. He is constantly acting out all that he imitates and imagines.

We have long recognized the educative value of play, and at no point is this more evident than with three-year-olds. The teacher's skill appears as she places in the child's path the materials that he will use in his play to make it most meaningful. For this reason the nursery teacher needs the right picture on the wall, and dolls and toys and picture books and blocks as standard equipment. If a child plays alone, or with another child, in a happy, friendly atmosphere, with a growing love for the church experience, he is growing in Christian nurture. There will be brief worship moments, but they will be informal and often in the middle of play. There may be an occasional story, very short, related to their immediate activities. For this kind of program the room should be sufficiently large, at least twenty-five square feet per pupil. There must not be overcrowding.

The good nursery room has various interest centers, such as an art center with paints and easel, a book table with little chairs, a music center where the piano is placed, a housekeeping center with dolls and equipment, a place where blocks are found, a nature center. At any center, a single child may be found, or two or three children together. Not all children are doing the same things at the same time.

How does the good leader teach the three-year-old? Or, to put it another way, how does learning take place?

The environment helps. We teach beauty and order only in the midst of beauty and order. Therefore, we try to have pleasing colors; a lovely picture hung at the right height and in the right light for the three-year-old; a sense of orderliness — children taught to work together in the cleaning-up process at the proper time. Little children are great imitators. They learn more from a teacher's happy disposition and courtesy to each one than from any amount of precept.

In their first year at church school we want children to cultivate a love for the church and a sense of its being their own. This comes, not from preaching or enjoining, but from pleasant experiences. The teacher teaches church loyalty by setting the stage for these happy experiences.

Much of the teaching is through the medium of guided activities. In their play at the various centers they are learning the beginnings of co-operation with other children. As a child paints at the easel he is learning free expression and a certain skill, and the leader has the opportunity of guiding the child into avenues of expression. Following the teacher's short and simple story, told perhaps to only three or four children at one of the centers, children may model figures in plasticene and play the story. If there is a plant to be watered, here is a chance for helpfulness in the group and for learning about the mysteries of nature. The child's activity must be in the form of participation, not mere observation; it must be his own free expression, not formal and dictated.

The nursery teacher is trying to guide the child toward growing co-operation and the beginnings of socialization. This is not easy at three. But it is part of Christian training — gradually to play and to live happily with others, to share with them, to be thoughtful of their feelings. One experienced worker with this age tells of setting up three simple rules:

1. Nursery class toys belong to everyone.
2. They must be shared. ("Now it is John's; soon it will be yours." Short, frequent turns are better for learning than long, infrequent experiences in sharing.)
3. Toys brought from home must be shared or put away with one's coat until taken home.[1]

All of this is a part of the teaching of religion, but the church nursery class has something more that the observer recognizes as being in the sphere of religion: a prayer that may be only a sentence; speaking of God as sending rain and sunshine; a simple, appropriate song; the presence of the Bible and occasional reference to it on the small child's level.

When a nursery teacher improves her techniques, it is very different from the way in which a junior teacher grows, but there is no less skill involved and what is done is of equal importance.

What has been said must make clear that a nursery class needs more than one leader. Because the child is so much of an individualist, personal attention is often required. When this is the case, another leader must be available for another child or for the group. The second person (or in a larger class, a third) may be an assistant or an apprentice in training, but in the nursery class dual or multiple leadership is important.

THE KINDERGARTEN AGE

The kindergarten teacher soon discovers how greatly children of this age vary among themselves, due in part to the homes from which they come and in part to the fact that the church experience is new to some, but not to all. Except in the small church,

[1] Gertrude Andon, *Nursery Children in the Church*. The Pilgrim Press, 1945, p. 17.

where combinations are necessary, teachers know that teaching will be easier if the four-year-olds and the five-year-olds are kept in separate groups.

Because children of this age learn by doing and observing, much more than by listening, the kindergarten teacher will have only a slightly more formal program than that of the nursery age. She will think more of well-planned experiences and organized activities than of a " lesson plan," as the teacher of an older group would use this expression.

To succeed as a teacher one must *make the child feel at home and happy in the church kindergarten*. Her aim is not to develop a child as a conformist but as one who feels at home in the church environment. This being the case, even the earliest comer must find a teacher at hand to greet him and he must feel that he has something to do at the moment he arrives. While children ten years old may all arrive at the same moment without any difficulty, the kindergarten class is fortunate if all its members do not come in together. An adjustment to one another and a constant feeling of at-home-ness is easier if the group grows slowly enough to become integrated easily. The kindergarten has an announced beginning time, but it must be thought of in a different way from that in which we think of a beginning time for an adult class; in the latter case, early-comers sit quietly and wait for the time to start. Kindergarten children must begin when they arrive. The teacher who expects the early-arriving five-year-old just to sit and wait will not only be disappointed but will also lose a good teaching opportunity. No one can be a good kindergarten teacher who plans to arrive just at the announced starting time. Thus there is very little formality about the session for four- and five-year-olds.

A second important point centers around the word " play." Much of the program is play, but there is not quite as much free play as at the nursery age, for now we find a slight move toward increased group activities. Even these have much of the play element. The planned activities are themselves a form of play — with blocks, with dolls, with paints, with singing.

A third point of importance has to do with " *interest centers*."

As in the nursery, the kindergarten teacher may arrange the room with an open space in the middle but with a number of centers of interest around the sides or in the corners: a music center, a building center where blocks are found, a library center where well-chosen books with pictures are kept, an art center where easel and paints are found, a beauty center that may or may not be called the worship center where a lovely picture or plant or flower may be placed. Children will spend part of their time at the center of their choice rather than with the entire group together, but not as much time as in the nursery class.

A fourth point the kindergarten teacher has in mind relates to the Bible. Very little use can be made of it, but still it has its place in the room and children discover that this is a special book in church or home. It is interesting to note what certain specialists in these early ages have said about the use of biblical material. While one authority tells us that at the nursery age there is no Old Testament story suitable and only four New Testament stories, another, speaking of the kindergarten age, finds eight suitable Old Testament stories and thirteen New Testament stories that are appropriate. The point here is that with kindergarten children, only a very few carefully selected biblical stories may be used in teaching. This is recognized in our better courses of study.

A fifth point to remember is that the kindergarten teacher attempts — though not by preachment — to guide the child as he begins to outgrow his earlier natural self-centeredness and show signs of a concern for something beyond himself. Note where the better kindergarten workers place the emphasis. They remind us that while some kindergartens always have children taking home things that show what they have done, the better ones inspire children during their free time at home or at play to find articles that the group is looking for to accomplish some school project. The church school, too, even at the early age of four and five, can begin to work against self-centeredness. When it does so it is engaged in good teaching.

Another way of teaching is through activity: informal dramatic play, painting, building, free drawing (not coloring within a pattern), modeling. The entire session may begin with this kind of activity for twenty minutes or so for those who come at the announced starting time, longer for those who come early, shorter for those who come later.

A seventh point of importance is that in the kindergarten, with all its free play and interest centers and individual activities, the casual observer is conscious of a program that seems more definitely planned than at the nursery age. The whole group may be together for a brief story, for singing, to look at a picture and to talk about it together, for worship — not formal, but spontaneous and at appropriate times, with a prayer (not addressed to Jesus but to God) which may be only a sentence and which may express a feeling of gratitude or appreciation. It is important that there be planned periods for conversation, in which teacher and children talk about everyday experiences.

Except in a very small church kindergarten class it is desirable to have more than one leader. The reason is that if the head teacher is busy with a single child or with a parent, there may still be sufficient supervision to insure a smoothly-running group.

In the kindergarten, children are learning gradually to love the church, to be happy in the new environment, to work and play harmoniously with others, to share with others, to widen their interests, to gain the first glimmering of a sense of God. To teach in the kindergarten calls for unique skills, an understanding of little children, and patience. But the teacher of young people who thinks that anyone can teach children four years old or five simply does not understand.

THE PRIMARY AGE

Teaching first-, second-, and third-grade children is markedly different from the task of teaching the pre-school ages. Probably these children have had kindergarten experience in the church or school or both, even if they have not been in a nursery class. At least they are in the elementary school during the week and learning to work as members of a group. They are not the individualists they were two or three years ago, and when they come to church school they come as members of a class — a group. The primary teacher differs from the kindergarten teacher in that she has a class to deal with, rather than a number of children who may be going in four directions at once.

For this reason the teacher of a primary class has a more clearly defined program — a course of study planned for all the members of the group, most of the time working together, or, if at times in separate groups, at least in a planned separation. This course of study may be on such a theme as " Stories of Jesus for Children " or " The Bells Ring Out " (about their church). But it is a real course to be taught to six- or seven- or eight-year-olds as a group. Because children of this age are capable of maintaining a sustained interest throughout a longer period of time, courses of study are frequently planned in units, each sufficient to continue through a number of sessions.

The good primary teacher has learned the importance of activities in teaching. It is fatal to success to suppose that one may adequately teach children of this age while they sit in a row as passive listeners. At no point in the church school is it more important for teachers to possess some basic skills of their own in the field of activities — so that they may know how to lead a class in informal, educational dramatization; so that they may know how to guide them in creative writing and expression; so that they may themselves possess the manual skills in drawing, painting, modeling, making notebooks, constructing friezes, sufficient to help children in these activities. For when we speak of " creative activities " we do not mean that children are left to flounder with no guidance, but rather that what they do shall not be dictated and stereotyped.

Such activities are not to be thought of as tacked on, after the completion of the lesson itself; they are an integral part of it. Sometimes they constitute the entire lesson. Sometimes all of the church school session may be devoted to such an enterprise, or at least a major part of it. Since there may be more learning from such activities than from a story told or from much talking by the teacher, they must themselves be regarded as part of the teaching process — not merely an adjunct to teaching. The good primary teacher knows how to guide pupils in such activities, and thinks of them as part of her central purpose for any particular unit of work. The seven-year-old is not like the nursery child, following his interest to the corner where the blocks are, or to the table where the books with pictures are found. These primary activities are chosen because they help the group to realize its purposes in this particular lesson or unit.

Primary children like stories. The good teacher therefore acquires skill in telling stories, carefully chosen for the age, related to the purpose of the course of study, longer than would have been appropriate at the kindergarten age.

Conversation is also important in the primary class. This may be thought of as elementary discussion; hence the primary teacher must school herself, not merely in talking *to* children, but in talking *with* them, drawing them out, so that everyone is participating in some way.

Good teaching at this age includes memory work — not as an assignment or a chore, but as an enrichment that an able teacher brings into the pupils' lives as they use beautiful and meaningful passages from the Bible, or the words of a song or hymn that are related to their course of study and used by the group in worship. As these hymns and passages become a part of their experience, memorization is easy, and sometimes almost unconscious.

At this age level there is such a thing as teaching outside the narrow limits of the course of study as usually interpreted. We teach by letting children have a part in doing things that traditionally the teacher has felt to be her own prerogative alone. Hazel Lewis tells about a primary superintendent who was always about forty-five minutes early in arriving so that she could have everything arranged " just so! " One Sunday, circumstances arose to make her very late (for her). A number of children were there, and she had to use their help. They were full of ideas and enthusiasm. For the first time, she saw the value of using them in an informal way to arrange a table, to get out some materials, to attend to this and that. Even if things were not in place as precisely as usual, the leader saw that the experience was giving the children a sense of participation and responsibility and joy; the emergency situation became a regular procedure.[2] We teach a child by giving him an opportunity to share in responsibility. Although we may not put this into practice as much as we should, its truth is obvious. Like the bride and groom who work for what they have and choose their own things to start out with, and thus get a thrill out of it that the other bride and groom miss when their misguided parents give them everything and even do the selecting of what they give — so the child cares more about a situation in which he has had a part.

Another way of teaching beyond the narrow limits of the course of study is through fellowship and service activities. Such experiences (see Chapter V) are most valuable. Better teaching calls for skill in carrying out enterprises of this kind.

On every hand we are reminded that a major trend of recent years is doing something about the fact that the home, more than the church, can be a teacher of religion. The leader who recognizes this and who, by any and all means, brings parents into a more active part in teaching religion to primary children is moving in the direction of better teaching.

THE JUNIOR AGE

Junior boys and girls are active. The successful teacher, then, must not expect them to be silent listeners. We can be certain that they will be active; the question is whether it is to be guided and purposeful activity or activity of quite a different kind. This is the reason why the junior teacher needs some of the skills discussed earlier in this book — skill in making a diorama, in construction, in notebook making, in dramatization, and the like

[2] See *The Primary Church School* (Revised) by Hazel A. Lewis, The Bethany Press, 1951, p. 120.

— so that he may use these skills in directing the pupil's activities in ways that will count in Christian nurture. Otherwise there will be activity — but of what kind?

The time-old parental question at Sunday dinner: "What did you learn today?" is ill-advised. The junior boy may not know what he has learned. He may have learned irreverence because of uncontrolled activities that are entirely out of place in the church, whereas planned and purposeful activities would have taught him something else. "What did you do today?" might reveal that he had learned something significant, if what he did was something in which he was deeply interested, something that gave him a new appreciation of the Bible, something in the line of service for a cause.

The junior's activity may take the form of investigation — not merely looking up something assigned by the leader, but investigating because he has the desire to find out. The teacher's art is shown in his ability to create the desire to discover, and this is a real art. A group of juniors who had just received their Bibles from the church had a teacher sufficiently skillful to lead them to a desire to know what was meant by all that was printed on the title page — "out of the original tongues," and so forth. A tremendous amount of investigation followed. This foresighted teacher had concordance, dictionary, Bible atlas, and different translations within easy access so that the desire to discover was not frustrated by any inability to proceed with the investigation. When boys and girls secure information in this way the good teacher will be sure to make use of it in the class; this impresses upon them the new learning and makes them regard investigation as worth-while and not futile.

Their activity may take the form of trips, out of session, but still a part and a rounding out of their class work. It may be a group excursion to a social center that will give them a background of understanding for a service enterprise; or a group visit to a Jewish synagogue, as a result of which intergroup fellowship may no longer be an academic question, but one that is rooted in experience.

Committee work may be an activity at the junior level, different from these other kinds, but of equal significance. For by the time pupils reach grades four, five, or six they are able to work together on committees for definite purposes — not too difficult, but really important. The reason some leaders hesitate at any such procedure is that they still think of teaching as talking, and still think that learning comes through listening, rather than through the personal effort and activity of the participant. A child may not accept a truth which he has merely heard, and his character is unlikely to be affected by hearing alone. But working at a task with one's fellows does produce learning and does have a definite effect upon character.

Interest groups at the junior age may also give a channel for purposeful activity. In an extended session of the department there is time for this kind of program—thirty or forty-five minutes for interest groups, one perhaps working on the department worship services, one concerned with a portrayal of the group's missionary activities, one dramatizing a favorite Bible story of the semester, one gathering and mounting great religious pictures for the picture file. Each chooses his own group. When boys and girls have worked together for a while in a task that is real and important, they have a sense of achievement.

Turning to the class session as it is usually conceived, the story is important at the junior age — not as an end in itself, nor as "the lesson," but as a means toward the end of realizing our objectives. Therefore the leader must acquire skill in storytelling. The art of group conversation is equally important at this age. Junior leaders sometimes make a distinction between discussion and conversation, saying that at this age they cannot be very successful with the former, but can be with the latter. The teacher must try to cultivate the art of leading a conversational group, assuming more leadership than would be necessary if they were three years older, and looking toward some definite findings or points of agreement as an outcome of the conversation, however simple the points may be.

The junior age has long been regarded as an appropriate time for memory work, even though it is not the only age suitable for this. One should not begin by making memory work a task or an assignment, but rather bring boys and girls to an understanding and appreciation of a great passage in the Bible, or a beautiful prayer, or a fine hymn, and use these so much that they are loved and unconsciously learned. The process may then be continued at home, where its continuance is more likely because pupils are then completing the learning of what they already love.

This is the first age at which the Bible occupies a significant place in the pupil's life. The primary child reads poorly and most of the Bible is too difficult for him. But when the church presents a Bible to a child — as it most frequently does at the end of the primary department, this is the time to help children to understand it, appreciate it, and use it. Junior classes, therefore, ought to use their Bibles. Very soon after children have received their Bibles from the church, it is desirable that their course of study help them to learn how to use these Bibles. Even if this is not the course itself, the teacher may well keep this thought in mind, so that as the year moves along, the pupils will be learning this very thing. In this way they will discover where their favorite stories are; they will learn how to find in the Bible what they want to find. In an elementary way, they will discover how the Bible came to be, the story of its translations, what is best suited for them to read, and how to begin to use it — not as they would read another book, starting at the beginning and continuing to the end, but by discovering stories that are most interesting and helpful to them, and the parts that fit in best with their Sunday morning studies. What point is there in presenting a Bible to a child, just as he is about to begin the junior department, unless the junior department experience will help him to know how to use it?

VIII

How to Teach Young People and Adults

Wнат is the difference between the way you teach junior high boys and girls and the way you teach those who are a little younger or those who are a little older? " I asked this question of one who has had wide experience with seventh-, eighth-, and ninth-graders. Her immediate answer was this: " You must have a sense of humor." She went on to explain that at this in-between age, when pupils do not want to be regarded as children, and when they are hardly young people in the technical sense, the effective teacher must have genuine understanding. Because this is a period of physical change and emotional upsets, and because the junior high youth is so often awkward and ill at ease, his leader must have sufficient sense of humor to meet him patiently in his varying moods. I put the same question to another person who has been an equally successful worker with this age. " You must treat them as more mature," she said — meaning more mature than boys and girls of the junior department, and more mature than they really are. This viewpoint is basic for the successful junior high leader.

This is a time when pupils need to straighten out their religious thinking. It is not enough that something has been taught them from infancy; now they begin to look critically at their Christian beliefs, and rightly so. What does the church teach about God, Jesus, prayer, the place of the church itself, and other important questions? And can they accept what they have always heard on these subjects? Some of the most valuable courses of study for the junior high age have been of this nature. Whether or not the course of study is in this area, the leader ought to be ready to discuss these themes with intelligent understanding and not be shocked if a pupil's ideas change often or differ markedly from what the leader regards as orthodox. The better teacher has convictions of his own, but is never so hide-bound as to be sure he has arrived at final truth. He is tolerant and patient when talking with his twelve- or fourteen-year-old pupil.

This is also the age at which we try to direct the pupil's thought toward the church and the Christian life. Many of us regard it as the most appropriate time to make a decision for the Christian life and to enter into church membership. Because the time is auspicious, we make plans toward this end. Church membership training classes have in them — and ought to have — more of the junior high than of any other age. Whether or not the curriculum includes a course on the church or the meaning of the Christian life, the leader will need to remember these emphases. Perhaps the most important point for a teacher to keep in mind is that the pupil's decision for the Christian life is essentially an acceptance of and commitment to Jesus' way of life rather than a subscribing to a creed or to a statement of beliefs. What, then, can be more important than that the junior high teacher help his students to know something of the life and teachings of Jesus so that, with understanding, they may accept him and commit themselves to his way of life? Whatever children's habits of church attendance or non-attendance may have been prior to this time, a teacher's aim may well be to establish church-attendance habits during the junior high period — ideally, each with one's own family; as a second choice, as a church school class group. It would scarcely be logical to have the time of church membership a time of non-attendance at the church's service of worship.

Junior high pupils need also to be introduced to great personalities. The regular curriculum will do this in part; but every good course of study needs enrichment, which can be achieved by the introduction of outstanding persons, past and present, who exemplify something of the spirit that is being stressed as religious truth. This is the period when, for the first time, boys and girls may come to appreciate the Hebrew prophets, and learn to know them as great exponents of social justice and concern for human values. This is the time when some of the great figures of church history — St. Francis of Assisi, Savonarola, Luther, Tyndale, and the like — ought to become living personalities. This is the time when outstanding missionary figures and leading Christians of other nations and races should become known and their contribution to the world appreciated. This is the time to guide young people of this age so that they will be alert to recognize Christian prophets and statesmen at work in the twentieth century.

At the junior high age we have a right to expect a more connected view of the Bible and a better understanding of the book as a whole. Some course of study ought to do this, helping the pupil to realize how the biblical literature was written and gathered together, to understand how it came to be " the Bible," and to know something of the story of its translations. The pupil ought also to get something of the sweep of the Old Testament and learn to understand the unity of the New Testament. Occasionally one finds a book that does some of these things for the junior high age. It is important that this over-all approach to the Bible be given to seventh-, eighth- and ninth-graders, partly because pupils are not ready for it any earlier and partly because, in all too many churches, unfortunately, boys and girls begin to disappear from the church school at the conclusion of this department.

The junior high teacher can use the discussion method more than it has been used at any earlier age. This is more than mere conversation; it is real discussion, with full pupil participation and with differing viewpoints presented and considered. If discussion is to be used, the leader must, of course, strive constantly to improve his skill and techniques in discussion leading.

Stressing the importance of discussion must not be interpreted as magnifying the place of talking in the class. It has its place, but not to the exclusion of activities. Some of the activities, such as trips to a settlement house or visits to synagogues or churches of quite different tradition become a basis for discussion. Dramatization is popular with this age, especially if pupils make their own play, based on an experience of their own or on some study they have been making. Thus, out of a study of the church, a group sometimes presents in dramatic form episodes in the story of their own church. Junior highs will make maps and models if they see a purpose in so doing. Notebooks have some point if they record what the group has done and discovered. The value of workbooks at this age is a mooted question; but some junior high leaders have found a fine response to the workbook idea, if it is not of the formal " fill in " type — and if boys and girls are in the mood for it!

One valuable activity for junior high students is that of planning their own programs, such as worship services. For this, creative writing (see p. 68) is appropriate and may be thought of as a creative activity within an activity. Planning service activities or fellowship experiences is equally important. The leader who always does this by himself has lost one of his best teaching opportunities.

YOUNG PEOPLE

The greatest difficulty in connection with the teaching program for the high school age and just above is that so often these young people are " among those absent." In conference after conference the question comes up: "Are you holding your young people? " A study of the churches of a certain area revealed the fact that about 50 per cent had a teaching program for the high school age and about 50 per cent had lost this group entirely. But they need the teaching ministry of the church as much as any other age.

Because of this difficulty some churches try to hold their young people by varying the program from the traditional pattern. They place less emphasis upon classroom courses, as such, and more emphasis upon group experiences and group activities. There is group worship and, necessarily, training in the leadership of worship. Meeting as an entire department, instead of dividing into classes, they may hear many excellent speakers. As an entire group, they engage in service activities, and enjoy many experiences that have educational value, as well as having the values that well-planned recreation gives. They may divide their membership into various committees for significant pieces of work.

Such a plan has its points of weakness and its points of strength. Its greatest weakness is that it lacks clear-cut teaching experiences. There is none of the give-and-take of classroom learning.

There are, however, compensating points of strength. Some churches have had the satisfaction of reaching a considerably larger proportion of the high school population of the community under this plan, than under the traditional plan of small classes within the department. Young people are still being trained in worship and in the leadership of worship. Through actual experiences, they are being trained in service and fellowship activities. In their own larger group, or in area conferences, they may be brought face to face with the question of Christian life service. Attendance at denominational or interdenominational summer conferences, with its recognized values, can be promoted equally well. There are assets as well as liabilities. We must not become so bound to a traditional pattern that we are unable to weigh values. Without a teaching program in the usual sense of the term, there may be many experiences through which learning takes place.

While at every age there is much teaching aside from that of the classroom and the course of study, this is more true of the high school age than of any younger period. At this age young people leave the home community to attend conferences and institutes of many kinds, and these are teaching experiences. They may work all day as a group, washing cars or raking lawns, all their earnings going to the missionary cause; if the work is properly followed up in their group meetings, the experience will teach them something about stewardship. If they entertain young people of other races and nationalities in their homes and at the church, the experience itself will teach more about the Christian spirit in intergroup relationships than much classroom talk could accomplish. They may lead services of worship, have a part in the youth choir, and engage in group worship; and these experiences teach them something of reverence and the reality of the unseen. We must not minimize the teaching value of planned and guided experiences apart from any course of study.

Fortunately, however, a large number of high school young people are still in church school classes, using definite courses of study. There should be more. How does the leader teach these classes? Not very often, it is hoped, by the lecture method; but in many and varied ways:

1. Before the course begins — or at the beginning of the course — it is possible to create an interest in the work of the year or semester ahead. A teacher may begin by helping the group to see the work of the term as a whole, and to realize how it fits in to their interests and experiences, so that it becomes an answer to their quest. It may be tied up with school work or with life problems, so that students look forward to it with expectancy. In some churches pupils of high school age — especially juniors and seniors — are given some choice in determining the course itself. Because they have a voice in deciding what it is to be, their interest and expectancy are greater. By way of example, one senior high class took one session to decide what their year's study would be. Under a competent leader, with the aid of a blackboard, they noted every area of study that they thought would be of value to a student by the time he had completed the high school department of the church school, and which seemed an appropriate theme of study in the church. In another column they noted all the areas of study, as far as they could recall, in which they themselves had engaged as church school members. It then appeared that there were three or four fields of study in their list which they had never touched. Of these, the one that caught their imagination most was " The Religions of the

World." That became their course for the year. And because they, themselves, had made the choice, their interest was all the greater.

2. *The use of available teaching aids* often makes a course interesting that otherwise would be drab. There ought to be a blackboard, fixed in the wall, or on a firm base (not the flimsy, rolling kind), with chalk and eraser always at hand. And it should be used. The church needs maps of Palestine, of Bible lands, of the world, of the United States, and at times special maps. If these are kept with other permanent supplies, the leader of a young people's class may borrow the one he needs on any given Sunday. So much is said and written today about visual resources that it is unnecessary to go into the matter here, except to suggest that the teacher of youth must know what these resources are and use them — not as substitutes for teaching, but as aids in teaching.

3. *The plan of occasional reports by members of the group,* as a result of their own investigation, makes them participants in the teaching task, helps in the learning process, and stimulates interest. The leader may need to remind, or assist, or furnish resources for such reports, but the extra effort will be justified by results.

4. *Class discussion* is important at this age (see Chapter IV), based on study or on a background of information secured in some other way. High school boys and girls are competent to participate well in discussion, holding to the subject, recognizing divergent points of view, and reaching conclusions; but they will do this only under the leadership of a teacher who has acquired some skill in discussion leading.

5. *The occasional use of tests* lends variety to the program, stimulates interest, and reveals differing attitudes, as well as knowledge or the lack of it. These tests may be of many kinds, for example, True-False, Social Distance, Multiple Choice, Attitude, Self-Rating tests, and so forth. A test may determine the procedure for a session or two. Its results may become the basis for group discussion. A test at the beginning of a course, repeated

toward the close, may reveal something of the group's progress in knowledge, or attitude, or point of view.

6. *The dramatic method* for the high school age will differ from the dramatic method for the primary age, but it can be equally effective. These young people may dramatize their own story or experience, informally, in the classroom. Using out-of-class time they may present a written play on a theme of value from the standpoint of their study — a Bible, missionary, race relations, or world peace play. As a group they may read such a play in a class session and use it as a basis for discussing a problem of Christian attitude or action.

7. What is done may be in the nature of a *group project*, so that the whole program of the class may be their own enterprise, initiated by them, determined by them, and by them carried to its logical conclusion. If the entire year's work cannot be conducted in this way it may be possible at many points for the leader to make use of the project method to such an extent that the class engages in its own activities, and its members feel themselves to be on the inside of the enterprise, following the line of their own interests and decisions.

What happens as a result of these class sessions? Surely, something. What happens is a test of the effectiveness of the teaching. This is not " applying the lesson " in a verbal and mechanical way. It has to do with changes in young people's thinking and insights and attitudes and character, so that things happen that otherwise would not have happened. As a course on the church proceeds, and after it is concluded, is there a deeper loyalty to the church and more devoted activity on the part of these young church members? After a course on missions, do we find a new group of young people committed to the world mission of the church? After a course on the Old Testament prophets, do we find a few high-schoolers with some convictions as to the social message of Christianity today? After a course on the teachings of Jesus, can we see any signs that the teachings of Jesus have become a standard of action for some of the sixteen- and seventeen-year-olds in the church?

Every so often someone is bold enough to assert that adult education is the most important opportunity of our time. And it is! If men and women will only continue their learning habits, they will discover that their capacity for mental growth is diminished scarcely at all as the years go by. Their learning ability is dependent chiefly upon their continuance of learning habits. Because of the influence and responsibilities of men and women in the church, the community, and the world of affairs, and because of the importance to themselves of enriching life to the end of life, adult study must be kept to the fore.

It would be unthinkable, therefore, to discuss the subject of teaching and stop with young people. We must include men and women. It is tragic for a church committee on Christian education to suppose it has fulfilled its function when it has provided for the better teaching of children and young people, without giving a thought to the religious education of adults. In many communities the church lags behind other agencies at this point.

On a recent visit to a Southern city I was shown through the educational building of one of the large churches. After seeing the facilities for children and young people, I became conscious of the fact that we were in a section of the building planned for men and women. The cards on the room doors made it clear that this church had many adult classes. Incidentally these classes were graded by age, as indicated by the notations to the effect that this one was " for ages 40 to 45," this " for those over 65," this " for ages 45 to 49," and so forth — a grading that few of us would be bold enough to attempt! I asked, " How many adults over twenty-one did you have present in classes last Sunday? " My guide answered, " We don't call them adults unless they are over twenty-four." " Then how many over twenty-four? " I asked. He consulted his notebook and answered, " Four hundred and eighty-seven men and women, in seventeen classes." This turned out to be almost exactly one-third of the total attendance of the church school for that Sunday. There was a church that regarded its teaching program as applicable to all ages, including men and women all the way from " twenty-four " to " over sixty-five."

In their national planning the Protestant denominations have attempted to go forward in adult education for some years, but the real problem is in the local church. In 1936, 1937, and 1939, significant conferences were held at Lake Geneva, Wisconsin, out of which grew the United Christian Adult Movement. One of the emphases was *Learning for Life,* a plan of adult study which took root in many places. It stressed the fact that men and women need to think and study in various areas — seven being outlined in the beginning: The Bible in Life; Personal Faith and Experience; Christian Family Life; Church Life and Outreach; Community Issues; Major Social Problems; World Relations. It gave many churches the idea that effective study might be, first in one of these areas, then in another, then another. Teaching is for adults, as much as it is for those who are younger. The church's teaching program includes enlisting men and women in different areas of study, according to their interests, out of which action may come.

If an adult study group is to be a success it must not look like a miniature church service. If the leader stands before a group and gives a lecture or a sermon, at the close of which the program is over, this can hardly be called a class or a discussion group. One of our chief dangers is at this point — that we will think we have an adult class when its members are mere listeners, and when the leader does nothing but deliver a lecture. We used to have many a " men's class " which was really a mass meeting, the program consisting of a hymn, a prayer, a lecture, and an adjournment — really competing with the church service of worship, and without any of the characteristics of an adult study group. As these mass meetings pass out of the picture it is with no great sense of loss. But unless their place is taken by real classes and discussion groups, there can be no sense of gain.

The good adult class may have such elements as these:

Its theme will represent an interest of the group. Theodore G.

Soares once wrote: " Many sermons are said to be ' over the heads ' of the audience. It would perhaps be more correct to say that they are aside from the interests of the audience." [1] Similarly a class theme ought to have some relationship to the interests of the class members. To make sure that this is so, a committee may plan to offer two or three courses simultaneously, from which people may choose; or from season to season the adult class theme may be changed from area to area; or the subject may be determined on the basis of an interest-finder, or some vote of expression on the part of the men and women of the church. Ideally we do not ask adults to " join a class "; we ask them, instead, on the basis of interest, to become members of a group that is to study a given theme that interests them.

There must be variety in the subjects of study — sometimes Bible study, sometimes mission study, sometimes a social issue or something on our Christian beliefs, sometimes a subject dealing with the home or world relations. Through a period of two or three years there should be evidence of comprehensiveness and variety.

It is a study class. To get something out of it, its members must put something into it. They do not constitute an audience; they are participants.

The time of meeting is determined by the matter of convenience. If the class meets on Tuesday evening, or on Thursday morning, it is as much a part of the church school as if it met on Sunday morning. If two courses are being offered during the same season, it is usually best to have them meet at different times, in order to suite the convenience of as many people as possible.

The extent of the course ought to be determined in the beginning and so announced. This is a three-month course or a six-week course or something else, with a given beginning date and a definite terminal date. This appeals to the modern busy adult who thinks he does not have time to enroll in a course that is to go on into the indefinite future.

[1] T. G. Soares, *A Study of Adult Life,* The Pilgrim Press, 1923, p. 54.

There is no one-and-only way of conducting an adult class session. Even the best technique calls for occasional variation. Consider a few:

1. *The lecture method.* Reference has already been made to this as an inadequate method. It loses sight of the needed give and take of group thinking. There are times, however, when this method has value. Sometimes there is a subject on which people need information, rather than the opportunity to express their own opinions. If a speaker has this information, there is value in having him give it. Even then, there should be ample time for questions and discussion. In most adult classes there is danger of overdoing the lecture method; it is to be used only when it serves a real purpose. Harry Thomas Stock expresses the idea well: "A steady procession of outside speakers makes for a lazy program, but an epidemic of discussions without occasional addresses by informed experts is likely to develop sophistication without wisdom." [2]

2. *The discussion method.* This is adapted to adult needs better than any other approach. It is imperative that the teacher of adults try to improve his skill in leading a discussion (see Chapter IV). One who has some ability along this line is sure to draw his class into participation often, whether or not the whole session is devoted to discussion. Almost every method has in it at least some place for the discussion technique.

3. *The panel discussion.* This may best be used in a large class. It does not mean a series of speeches by the members of the panel. It should be thought of only in the technical sense of the term: a statement of the case by the chairman, with the problem at issue clearly defined — a problem on which there are varying points of view; a discussion by the members of the panel — back and forth in a conversational way; opening up of the subject to the whole group for comment, question, and discussion; and a concluding summary by the chairman.

4. *Reports* from members who have accepted previous assign-

[2] Harry Thomas Stock, *Young People and Their Leaders,* The Pilgrim Press, 1933, p. 67.

ment and made preparation. This brings more people into significant participation and adds to the class interest — if it is not done too often. A needed caution for the leader is this: when you make an assignment, give a time limit and hold to it.

5. *The question box.* This is a welcome method provided it is used but rarely and provided also the person chosen to answer questions is adapted to the task and is one who has the respect of the group in the particular fields of thought being considered.

6. *The group at work on its own statements* — of belief, of social ideals, of Christian purpose, of missionary program, and so forth. This is a form of group discussion, calling for decisions every step of the way. It requires a leader who not only can lead group discussion, but also can sense the group mind, and interpret it.

7. *Reading and conversation.* Sometimes a study of one of the Gospels lends itself to the plan of spending a few sessions in which passages of Scripture are read by blocks or wholes (not verse by verse), so that all may get an appreciation of it and enjoy the advantage of group conversation — as in anyone's living room — on this piece of biblical literature.

8. *Investigating committees working on specific problems.* This may be a between-session activity of finding out more in regard to the outreach of the church (as in a missions course); of discovering what the creeds have said or what their own denominational statement is on a given subject (as in a course on Christian beliefs); of tracing out the facts regarding Bible translations (as in a course on the Bible through the centuries); of gathering statistics regarding expenditures for liquor and its relation to crime (as in a course on the liquor question). Such activities enlist the participation of many members of the group and furnish factual material for informed discussion.

To enlist and to hold men and women in adult classes, we need the conviction that they are ready to respond to a carefully worked out plan; we need an appealing program; and we need leaders who are ready to vary their approaches and to improve their techniques, as they take their part in the teaching work of the church.

IX

What About Discipline?

Iᴇ it were not for the matter of discipline, I would be willing to take a church school teaching job." " I worry a lot about discipline, but Mr. Gray never seems to think about it and yet his class gets along beautifully." " When I visited my child's Sunday School, the noise was terrible; no discipline at all!" " Have you noticed that Miss Clark never seems to have any disciplinary problems? Everything seems to move along smoothly and happily. Yet last year that was our problem class." Comments of this kind have a familiar ring. What is commonly called " discipline " is the nightmare of many an untrained worker asked to teach in the church school.

The difficulty seems to stem, in part, from a tradition of Sunday School disorder. But we must also recognize that in many places there is no such problem, and a counter-tradition has grown up of a smoothly-running school, with happy and eager group participation, and with the word " discipline," in this sense, almost eliminated from the worker's vocabulary.

The difficulty arises also from the fact that the majority of teachers are volunteers and untrained; but the movement for training volunteer workers on the job has made tremendous strides in the last generation. This has had its influence on the quality of the teaching; and better teaching is always accompanied by a lessening of the disciplinary problem.

A third reason sometimes given for this problem is the fact that the church school lacks the authority of the public school and must, therefore, be more lax. It happens, however, that the public school itself — with its " authority " — sometimes faces serious disciplinary problems, and it also happens that the church school

— without authority — sometimes furnishes examples of excellent classroom procedure so that one does not even think of the word "discipline." All of which points to the fact that there may be something more important than so-called external authority.

The best way to attack this problem is to attack its causes. This is one reason why this book does not begin with this chapter but, instead, with other emphases which, if properly made, will automatically reduce the causes of so-called disciplinary problems. The inexperienced teacher may suppose that one of his first problems is that of classroom behavior; but he is bound to learn, whether easily or the hard way, that this is not true at all. Good advice for a beginning teacher is this: *Try to avoid disciplinary problems rather than learn how to meet them.*

When one looks objectively at a teaching situation and sees unsatisfactory behavior on the part of the pupils, it is natural to try to analyze the situation to discover the reasons. Such reasons as these may appear:

1. The quality of the teaching may be poor.
2. Nothing may be done to catch the interest of the pupil.
3. The teacher may not understand what is meant by the democratic method in teaching.
4. The room conditions may be unsatisfactory.
5. The school may not yet have succeeded in securing satisfactory home co-operation.
6. For some reason or other, individual boys and girls may have a sense of insecurity.
7. We may be thinking of discipline as something imposed from without, rather than as something that has to do with a pupil's inner feelings or purposes.
8. There may be a lack of rapport between teacher and pupils; they may not be on friendly and understanding terms with one another.
9. The difficulty may lie in the program itself.
10. Some pupils may be non-co-operative and really obstreperous!

The chief danger which the inexperienced group leader faces is that of assuming that his problems stem from the tenth point, not from some of the other nine. From any one of these ten causes, however, and no doubt from others as well, a situation may arise that results in what is commonly described as bad discipline. Obviously the pupil is not responsible for every such state of affairs; then why blame him? Why attempt to tackle the question of unco-operative behavior by itself as if it had no cause other than an evil disposition in a particular child?

The first point to stress, therefore, is that we must emphasize the positive — not the negative. Leaders in the field of pedagogy have discovered that a child learns more from the activities in which he is permitted to engage than he does from the activities which he has been stopped from doing. The distressed leader is constantly saying, " Don't do that! " because he has not opened up sufficient oportunities to do such things as he would like to see him do. It is the appreciative teacher who will take the latter course. The one who has been able to open up no new avenues of pupil activity will be driven to the negative course and will become more of a fault-finder.

A second point to stress is that the best way to solve disciplinary issues is not to attack them head-on, but to go back to causes. If the leader can make some improvement in the first nine of the ten points listed above, the major part of our problem will vanish. We would not have a high regard for the medical profession if it dealt merely with symptoms, and not with causes. Why should we have any higher regard for teachers who begin at the point of discipline, which is usually a symptom, and make no effort at all to correct the situations which are the causes of the misbehavior that bothers them?

A third point to stress is that we beware of the easy and super-ficial ways of meeting behavior problems that do not solve them at all. One such way is by means of rewards. Those who " behave themselves " (which usually means those who conform to our pattern, or who do not disturb us, however passive and non-creative they may be) will get a book or a box of candy! That is merely a bribe. It does nothing to help us reach our basic aims; it does not change character; it is merely an exchange of a desired object for a forced pose. Another easy way of meeting behavior problems is to send a child from the room. This is a negative approach. It relieves the teacher of an unpleasant situation for the moment, but it is no solution of the difficulty. A teacher sometimes worries as to whether she ought to send a child home or to the superintendent, when the thing she ought to worry about much more is how she can improve her teaching techniques to capture that child's interest and co-operation.

Let us consider in more detail the ten situations mentioned above out of which disciplinary difficulties often arise:

1. *If I have serious disciplinary problems in my class the first thought in my mind ought to be: Perhaps the quality of my teaching is poor.* The proof that a major portion of such problems vanishes as one's teaching skill increases is found in the fact that the better teachers have the fewest problems of this nature.

It may be partially a matter of poise, calmness, and manner. The one who is well poised, who does not begin until he has everyone's attention, who so keeps an eye on every member that no one gets away from him for a moment — such a teacher has a marked advantage, as a disciplinarian, over the nervous type of leader who begins a class session while half the members are still engaged in conversation. For children tend to reflect a teacher's attitude. If he is tense, they become so. If he is unorganized, they easily become disorganized. They respond in kind to his mood and manner.

The previous chapters of this book discuss some of the ways in which we may work toward better teaching: planning well for Sunday morning; having everything in readiness when Sunday morning comes; being growing, alert persons; developing skill in storytelling, in leading conversation and discussion, in using informal dramatization as a teaching method, in utilizing many and various forms of creative activity, in leading the class in service and fellowship projects, in improving our method for the particular group we teach. Such areas as these are the ones in which

to work and the fields in which we must make improvement,
if we are to reduce the nuisance of poor discipline.

No normal, healthy twentieth-century child can be expected
to sit through an hour's class session as a passive listener. The
child must do things, be a participant, feel himself an active part
of the teaching period, and the teacher who does not plan for
him to be that kind of class member is inviting difficulty.

So often we blame children for something that is no one's fault
but our own, as teacher!

Teacher was late. Everything had happened. Now it looked as if this
was one of those days in Church school. The children were running, shouting
and laughing. Teacher was angry. Her voice was very sharp.

The children listened, looked at her wonderingly, and for a moment
became very still.

Tommy wondered, " Gee, what was so wrong about that? Can't a guy
have a little fun? Class hadn't started anyhow. . . ."

But now there were some things to do and Tommy liked the things his
class was doing.

As Teacher thought about the day, she remembered that she had been
late. She had not provided anything for early comers and certainly she did
not expect them to sit still. She remembered that many ill feelings had gone
to class with her. She wondered — Why had she been so angry with the
children? The children had wondered too! [1]

2. *If I seem to have disciplinary problems in my class, perhaps
what I have been doing has failed to enlist the pupil's interest.*
This, of course, is related to the first point: the leader who fails
to take into account the child's interests is to that extent failing
as a teacher. It has well been said that the bored class is the
problem class; when there is an undisciplined group the fault may
not lie chiefly at the door of the members of the group itself, but
with the leader who has failed to build on interest.

Participation is often the key to interest. One who feels himself
to be on the inside of an enterprise has a concern for its success.
There's a vast difference between being on the outside, observing
what is done, and being on the inside as one of the planners and

[1] From *Discipline in the Church School,* a mimeographed document prepared
and published by The Children's Committee, Ohio Conference of Congregational
Christian Churches.

doers. Activity is a key to interest. Pupils who are at work making a diorama, those who are busy in a service enterprise, boys and girls informally dramatizing the story of Joseph, a group in creative writing preparing a litany for a worship service — these are almost always so interested in the activity itself that any tendency to be non-co-operative or to disturb others is at a minimum. In other cases there may be no such activity, manual or otherwise. Instead, the class may be engaged in a conversation, of interest to them, in which the teacher does not talk all the time but has the faculty of drawing out members of the group and utilizing the various contributions they make. In this, interest can be just as real as in a period of manual activities, with disciplinary dangers just as unlikely. The good leader tries to discover the pupil's basic interests, but also to lead them into new and important interests, by techniques that are interesting in themselves.

3. *As the group leader I may not understand what is meant by the democratic method in teaching.* Or if I know, as one often knows a textbook, I may not have the disposition or the ability to put my theories to work; I may not use the democratic process.

Some of us have recollections of a semi-military regimentation in the classroom for periods of time when everyone was required to " face front — with hands behind." It is a long way from that to the state of freedom, with order, in the modern well-regulated day school or church school. I am thinking of a church school junior group in which everyone was at work on his own project. Each pupil on arrival went to the shelf where his own materials were kept, brought them out and went to work, for that was the way the session started. There was no pin-drop silence in the room; each one was interested in his neighbor's work as well as his own, and neighbors would often discuss what both were doing.

If we are to prepare children for democratic living we must use the democratic procedure in the classroom. More decisions must be made together, rather than by the teacher alone. The group must plan and their voices must count in decisions reached. Pupils may have a part in preparing the room; they may decide whether to use a flower or a Bible or a picture on the worship center; in their giving " for others," they may have two or three causes brought to their attention, express preferences, and decide in a democratic way the cause to which their gifts are to go; in a group discussion, under the teacher's guidance, they may set their own goals on all sorts of questions, such as group behavior, parties and social events, and the condition in which they will leave their classroom in fairness to the sexton or to the class that follows. The mere fact of participation in setting such goals insures greater effort in reaching them than if everything had been decided arbitrarily by the leader .

To a degree, the same principle holds true in the evaluation of the work of the class or of its various members. Constructive criticism by the group is good, with more emphasis on appreciation than on weaknesses, but always with the leader keeping control. If the group evaluation has to do with non-co-operation on the part of some of its members, it may be democratic to get different opinions and viewpoints, but the leader will have to remember that children can be unjustifiably severe in passing judgment on one another, and therefore final decisions cannot always be left in their hands. When a leader discusses discipline with a class, his purpose is to seek their help, advice and co-operation; he is not turning everything over to them, on the one hand, nor, on the other hand, is he laying down the law himself.

The democratic method does not require that children be permitted to make all decisions by themselves, without leadership or guidance. That right belongs to them only so far as they are able to use it. In our political life we place brakes upon freedom: one does not vote until a given age; even Congress does not have a free hand in everything; if its action is unconstitutional there is a higher authority so to declare it; in certain situations the majority does not rule; on the other hand, the Constitution gives every citizen certain rights that no one can take away. Apply all this to children in the church school. The democratic method means that children are brought into the planning and deciding stage, but within certain limitations. It means that they make an increasing number of decisions, but not beyond their ability, and with their teacher as a member of the group, to guide discussion in such a way that when decisions are made the children feel them to be group decisions. Certainly the democratic method means that a teacher disclaims the role of authoritarianism and tries more and more to bring the pupil into the planning, the deciding, and the evaluating of the whole enterprise.

4. *If my class has problems of discipline, the trouble may be due to the conditions of the room itself.* One should analyze one's own situation to discover whether there are any factors of this kind and whether they can be corrected, even in part.

A common difficulty is poor ventilation. This is a weakness that is easy to correct and one that should be on the teacher's mental checklist; for a close, stuffy room reflects itself in uncomfortable and irritable children — and teacher, too!

Inadequate provision for wraps is another cause of a situation that is easily interpreted as poor discipline. When boys and girls keep coats on, and have no place to put their hats, the psychological effect is bad; it creates the impression of haste and transiency; there is no feeling of a work period such as is created when hats and coats have been deposited at some proper place, leaving pupils in the mood of readiness for participation in a class enterprise.

All too many classrooms — or class meeting places — are messy and untidy. It is a law of life that we reflect our environment, and that kind of class setting is bound to be a factor in producing careless and ill-mannered behavior. Pupils who are given an untidy and ill kept place to meet cannot be blamed for behavior that corresponds to the surroundings. Fortunately, this is a situation that can easily be corrected. The class quarters of many a church school need an old-fashioned house cleaning.

No teacher can be blamed for the fact that her class is one of ten in a big assembly room — each gathered about a table and all subject to one another's hubbub. Lack of finances may be at the root of the difficulty. Instead of criticizing the badness of the younger generation in being so noisy and so undisciplined, the church itself should do something about it: perhaps a campaign for improved equipment, with volunteer labor; perhaps an effort to find another place — a renovated, unused room, a reclaimed and remade basement area, space in the parsonage or another nearby home — for even one of these classes, or for two.

An overcrowded classroom increases the likelihood of non-co-operation and misbehavior. Don't blame the boys and girls; they are just as human as you were at their age. Divide the group, forming another class, and thus reduce the disciplinary problem.

The room may not be crowded but still the group may be too large for one teacher without assistants. With a large room, you need not make two classes out of one, for the trend is toward larger classes. Secure an assistant teacher, or two if necessary — a parent, or a young person who has just graduated from high school and for whom such an apprenticeship will be real training — and thus change an unwieldy group into one that operates smoothly.

At the other extreme, the membership of a class may be too small. It needs the inspiration of numbers to develop the spark of interest and thus to overcome listlessness or disorder. Combining two classes on a group-graded basis may help, if attempts to recruit new members do not succeed.

The equipment may be such that there is scarcely any opportunity for planned activity of any kind, making the class merely a listening group. This is an invitation to trouble. A work table suggests something besides listening. In addition to this, if a class has room to move about, there is opportunity for various forms of activity that may not only counteract poor discipline but also make possible a better quality of Christian education.

5. *The disciplinary problems I face may reflect inadequate home conditions.* This does not mean homes that lack wealth, or homes that lack education. It means homes that lack a religious concern, or homes that have no thought of co-operation with the church in a common teaching task.

The solution is not the task of a day, but a long and continuous effort. One of the most fruitful approaches is that of enlisting parents in activities related to the church and its school, even though their co-operation at first may seem to be of only minor significance. The parent who is doing even a little for the educational program of the church begins to have a growing concern that this program run smoothly, especially in so far as his own child is concerned.

Another important approach — whether or not leaders are conscious of disciplinary problems — is an occasional friendly conference of teacher with parents, whether in the home or anywhere else, when a teacher is not complaining about a child's attitude but seeking advice and trying to discover wherein he, the teacher, is falling short or failing to do all that he should do.

Still another approach is to find ways of helping the home to engage in some of the practices and co-operate in some of the activities that are in line with our aims in Christian nurture. As a single illustration, one church school [2] sent to the homes at the beginning of the Advent season a simple but attractive eight-page folder on "Family Worship Through the Christmas Season," with a page for each Sunday and one for Christmas Eve — each page being what one family in the church had done, with the name of the family given: a carol, a poem, a prayer, perhaps an interpretation, with each child and parent participating. It was a way of suggesting to all the homes of the parish what had come out of particular homes in that very parish.

Perhaps the best word to parents can be spoken by a fellow-parent, "as one parent to another." In the document already referred to (page 124), *Discipline in the Church School*, a page, signed by a parent, is called "A Parent's Perspective." "Have I done my best," the writer asks, "toward helping my child learn?" As one parent to another the writer can say what teachers could never say: "We, as parents, owe a debt of gratitude to those who willingly give of their time and thought and energy for our children."

6. *If my class presents disciplinary problems, the difficulty*

[2] The First Church in Newton, Massachusetts, at the beginning of the Christmas season, 1954.

may lie in the fact that on the part of one pupil or two there is some feeling of insecurity. A child's world includes his home, his school, his church, his free time at play, and other experiences as well. But in these different environments he does not always meet with the same control; there is an inconsistency in the various areas of his world that adds to his difficulties and makes him feel insecure. Sometimes it seems as if he is free to make his own rules and follow his own whims; sometimes it seems as if he is living under rigid control; sometimes it seems as if there is little consistency even within just one of the various domains in which he lives — home or school or church: free and lax one day, hard and rigid another.

The fine line between freedom and control is always difficult to draw. We want children to have freedom enough for them to develop initiative and not to smother spontaneity and creativity. Not every movement and decision of the child is to be dictated. On the other hand, however, without some rules, some authority, some control we are denying the child the training he needs and keeping him in a state of insecurity.

Every child must learn that there are certain " rules of the game " that must be followed. Some things are not matters of debate. In certain areas there is definite authority. Even adults are in identically the same situation: we may not park in certain places; nor dump our tin cans in the street; nor build on our own property contrary to the zoning laws. The majority of citizens have a respect for the law, knowing that it is for the common good for all to be under the law. The younger generation, too, must grow up into this same attitude — that some things are not done, that some things are contrary to the rules of the game, that in some areas of life we cannot follow the " do as we please " philosophy. Boys learn this early in baseball. In well regulated homes, children learn it up to a certain point (even though it is with some struggle): if eight o'clock is bed-time, this ceases to be a matter of argument; in one room there are things we do not do; on school days home is the place to be in the evenings; each one makes his own bed. In school there may be considerable freedom, but still, for the common good, there are rules of the game: we arrive at a fixed time in the morning; we do not straggle in when we choose; instead of all talking at once we have some regulating rule. Because there are some basic rules in home and school and at play the child knows what to expect and this gives him a sense of security.

The same must be true in the church school; some basic points must be recognized: we are there at beginning time; each one has work to do; in a worship service everyone's attitude is that of quiet reverence and group participation; no one talks while another is speaking; a certain respect — even though in the spirit of comradeship — is due the teacher. There must be some authority and some recognized rules, for utter freedom becomes chaos. The pupils themselves ought to have a part in making such rules. Not only is this an important experience in their own training, but rules will be better respected if those who are to follow them have helped to make them. Just as a person who lives under law in a civilized community feels secure, so the one who recognizes some basic law — some rules about which there is no question — has a feeling of security, at church as well as at home or in school or at play. Under this kind of law there is still ample room for initiative and freedom of choice and creativity.

If a child is to have this sense of security, he must find consistency in the operation of the rules of the game. At his school, he does not find that he is expected to be on time on Monday but that on Tuesday it makes no difference. In his home if the rules of the game call for bedtime at eight on Wednesday, with no rule at all on Thursday, he becomes confused and his sense of security begins to wane. At church also there must be consistency: group rules and expectations of this month must hold next month also. Just as civilized society has some controls and regimentation for all of us, so the church — like the school and the home — must have some fixed controls for the sake of the child's mental ease and security, as well as for the sake of a smoothly-running institution. The child who has no controls is unpleasant to have around and unhappy in his own life. There are some areas in which we do not give a child a choice, any more than his parents have a choice when they drive up to the red light. There are some phases of life in which the younger generation must be taught to conform; and the reason for conformity is partly for the sake of the group, but partly to give a sense of security to the individual.

7. *The difficulty may lie in the fact that I am thinking of discipline as something imposed from without, rather than as something that has to do with a pupil's inner feelings or purpose.* Our aims in education (Christian or otherwise) include the child's growth and development. We want him to mature. If he is maturing, he is coming to see the reasons for his actions, to choose between different courses of action on the basis of the directions in which they will lead, and to assume the qualities of a more responsible member of society. When a child begins to make decisions for himself, when he acts in class on the basis of something within himself, when he makes choices in the direction of a spirit of co-operation in the group or in the direction of a certain way of life because of an inner purpose — then we have some assurance that he is maturing. Moving in this direction, a boy shows signs of what may be called self-discipline. His own inner feelings and purposes are determining his actions, not some outward authoritarian control.

This is highly to be desired. If a girl continues to " behave," year after year, simply on the basis of conformity to the demands of a teacher who lays down the law and requires silence now, and doing things as directed at another time, she has no more chance of maturing than she would have in a home in which, even up through the teens, a parent's word is law, not to be disputed or questioned. The leader who is concerned for a pupil's growth in self-discipline will care less about his own authority and think less about obedience to his own commands; on the other hand he will think more about what is happening in the inner life of the pupil — his motivation for his behavior, his ability to choose between divergent courses of action, his attitude and the inner feelings back of his action. The good leader does not merely ask whether the pupil is refraining from annoying others, whether he is acting as he has been bidden to act, whether he is conforming to adult demands. The problem goes deeper. The good leader is concerned about what is happening within the child — his attitudes, his interests, his desires, his judgments.

The better teacher is not looking primarily for a silent group member who never disturbs, nor for a mere conformist; but for one who may not always conform because he is maturing, making decisions of his own, and learning to act as a responsible person who enjoys the degree of freedom for which he is prepared. One factor that multiplies disciplinary problems with some of us is that we still think of discipline as something imposed on the child from without, rather than as something that has to do with his inner self and that reflects the degree of his maturing.

John Dewey once said: "Discipline is a product, an outcome, an achievement, not something applied from without."

8. *If my class presents diciplinary problems, it is possible that the difficulty may root back into the feelings of the boys and girls who are not receiving the love and understanding that everyone craves and needs.* If I am conscious of turmoil and misbehavior in my class one Sunday, the difficulty may be traced, not to anything that happened that Sunday, but to what happened or did not happen during previous weeks and months. If I had been cultivating the friendship of this girl who seems most obstreperous this week; if I had manifested a little love for this boy and concern for his interests from the beginning of the year, perhaps there would be no outburst this week. This means that in my whole attitude and manner through the year there is a preventive power. When Sunday's outburst comes we blame this boy or that girl for their actions, when perhaps we should blame ourselves for failing to cultivate this boy or girl throughout the year and to show more friendship and affection. Perhaps this is what some psychologists mean when they say that discipline in a class has to do with the teacher's attitude and action in peaceful moments as well as at times of storm and stress. A pupil is most likely to be co-operative in the class, and to be in the learning mood, when

his feeling for his teacher is one of friendliness and affection, with the desire to co-operate and to be helpful. A disciplinary problem, therefore, may have its source in the leader's actions or neglect of the past, not in any situation of this particular class session. The whole issue of discipline must be placed on a long-range basis; it is not merely a question of what is happening today.

9. *At least a part of my disciplinary difficulties may have their source in the program itself.* A lack of co-operation and what we regard as misbehavior may be a reflection of *curriculum materials unsuited* to the particular class. If the classroom curriculum is too advanced for these pupils, or too simple for them, or outside the range of their interests, we may expect to encounter disciplinary problems. It is easy, however, to put the blame on the course of study when it belongs elsewhere. For this reason I must not take my own judgment as final; if I think the course of study inappropriate, while two other teachers, using the same materials with the same age, get along admirably, the chances are that my judgment is faulty; we had better have objections from more than one before disregarding material as unsuited for the age for which it has been prepared. Because one teacher has behavior problems while teaching a certain course, we must not think we have sufficient ground for putting the blame on the curriculum. There are instances, however, when the materials used are at fault.

There are also times when the difficulty lies in the fact that a teacher is given inadequate curriculum helps. In our efforts to encourage leaders to be free and creative we sometimes adopt a policy of giving them a theme, with practically no prepared and clearly outlined course. This is a mistake. The average volunteer teacher needs something specific; within that definite pattern there is still ample room for originality and creativity. But to turn an untrained teacher loose, without a course of study that gives careful guidance and possible procedures, and to do so in the name of creativity is inexcusable; in fact it is itself bad pedagogy, for it is attempting to push people faster than they are able to go. In such a case, it is not the course of study that is to blame, but rather the lack of any such course.

The program of the department *beyond the class session*, or the lack of any such program, may be to blame for our difficulties. Are there any service activities that go over into the week? Is there ever an extra session of the group for a purpose recognized and felt by the class itself? Are there occasional recreational opportunities that bind the class and its leader together? If there is never a single planned experience beyond the Sunday morning hour, that may be at the root of the trouble. If there are activities that are too simple, or unsuitable, or dictated with no pupil determination, the difficulty may lie there.

The *grouping* may be unsatisfactory. In a very small school it may seem necessary to have a wide age range in a single class, but even there, division may prove desirable, for classes may grow if they are more homogeneous. The small school does well to list its constituency for each grade (sometimes only one pupil) and to secure expert advice from a denominational office as to the most satisfactory way of grouping them in classes. In larger schools there is occasionally too much carelessness as to grouping, which breeds trouble in the field of discipline — when too little attention is paid to school grade and too much left to chance or whim.

Thus it is possible that the cause of some of our disciplinary problems may be found in the program itself. If this is true, the way to find a solution is not to attack the problem head-on but to remove the cause by correcting the program.

10. *If I face disturbance and marked lack of co-operation in the class, this may be due to none of the reasons mentioned; it may be that someone is showing his worst side; it may be a situation that must be dealt with then and there.* Only rarely is misbehavior due to causes other than the nine mentioned above or others closely related to them. Usually misbehavior is a result of poor teaching or some of the other factors already considered. It behooves us, therefore, to center our efforts on such points as these rather than to begin with " discipline." Everyone recognizes that the best teachers have the least difficulty. If we are doing what we can to have the best possible room conditions and the best home relations, we may double our efforts toward train-

ing teachers in better methods, better understandings, and better techniques and then watch disciplinary problems fade into the background. This cannot be said too emphatically. It still remains, however, that even the good teacher occasionally will face a critical disciplinary situation.

One's rule should be: " This I will not tolerate; I must do something about it at its first appearance. If I do not do something about it now, the situation will get out of hand. My first concern is that I find a way of protecting the larger group of pupils, and not let this incident disrupt their learning."

On the negative side, one must be careful not to follow a course that is an admission of defeat, such as sending the disturbing child home, or to a superintendent, or out of the room. Occasionally one finds a church school that sets up its machinery for just such a procedure, with a monitor in the hall in case a child is sent out, or with a person in an office to whom culprits may report.

Setting up machinery of this kind reveals the expectation that it is going to be used and serves as an encouragement rather than a deterrent to misbehavior; it also serves as an invitation to a teacher to take the easy course of sending out a pupil since someone is waiting outside to catch him!

Occasionally it may happen, with an inexperienced teacher, that outside help will be needed and that someone in authority — or someone with more authority — may be brought into the class for a while to assist. In the long run, however, the person who handles a situation himself will be better satisfied than if he had thrown its solution onto other shoulders.

If a class session is in danger of being disrupted by a " smart aleck " or a boy in a disturbing mood, a leader may often cure the difficulty by stepping up to this one, standing by him, but continuing to talk or having the class continue in its work. If one is giving an explanation or telling a story when the disturbance begins, one may continue but all the time keep one's eye on the offending pupil. If this does not work, and if the class is in the midst of a group discussion, the leader may direct a question toward this same pupil. If possible, bring him back into his place in the group by focusing attention upon him, but without interrupting the course of the class session.

There are times, however, when this is not enough. It may be necessary to pause long enough to isolate the offender — if the room is sufficiently large — giving him a job to do by himself. This must be a real job — something that has value in itself — not something that is mere punishment; it may be a book to read on which he will be asked to report later; it may be some creative activity to complete, but something that is a part of the work of the class.

If two are pommeling each other during a group conversation or discussion period, it must not continue, for if it is allowed to continue it will be repeated often. There are times when it becomes necessary to pause in one's planned session to discuss with the whole group the matter of making their own rules for the conduct of the class. There are some " rules of the game " that they may work out for themselves as to having only one talk at a time, consideration for others, class procedures. The group that makes its own rules is most likely to abide by them.

If some unpleasant experience has occurred during any session, it should not be forgotten when the end of the class session comes. Right then is the time for teacher and problem-boy or problem-girl to sit alone for a few minutes, after the others have gone — not for threats or punishment, but for a friendly talk on ways of working together to make the class better. This is the time to give the offender some responsibility for the following Sunday. This is the week to try to see him in a casual way to develop his friendship. This is the time for a talk with his parents — not in complaint or fault-finding, but as a teacher who needs advice, a teacher who has not yet succeeded in finding the right way with their child and who therefore needs their help.

There must be freedom in our classes. But how much? Some boys and girls are so constituted that they will take all the freedom the teacher allows. There must, therefore, be freedom under control — freedom within the law. But there must be some law, some rules, some understanding as to what is done and what is not done if the class session is to be a learning experience. There must be a recognition of the fact that freedom ceases to be freedom, and becomes lawlessness, if it hinders others from making progress in this learning experience.

In conclusion, and at the risk of needless repetition, the place to begin is not with the problem child, or the question of discipline, or what to do when someone disrupts the best laid plans. The place to begin is with the cause of such a situation. Don't blame the child; ninety per cent of the time the cause lies somewhere else. Is the policy of the school and of its teachers such as to bring to pupils a feeling of happiness, a consciousness of being appreciated, a sense of security? Are efforts being made to help homes to take their part in Christian nurture? Are the equipment and the physical surroundings the best that they can be? During the class session are the members of the class doing things themselves, as participants, in which they are interested — not merely sitting as silent listeners? Is the church using every means at its disposal to improve the quality of the teaching?

The more often a teacher has to discipline a pupil, the greater should be that teacher's sense of defeat. For we solve this problem, not so much by attacking poor discipline head-on, as a thing by itself, but rather by setting out consistently on a campaign to remove its causes.

X

How Do We Know
When Teaching Is Good?

FEW QUESTIONS are more difficult to answer, for this is a field in which measurement is not easy. We may have an excellent educational building, with well-equipped classrooms, but still our teaching may not be a success. A good building and a fine classroom, however, ought to make it easier to be successful in teaching. We may have the best possible curriculum materials, up-to-date audio-visual resources, blackboards and activity equipment, and still our teaching may not be good. Such materials, however, are important and make good teaching easier. Attendance may remain at a high level and still our teaching may not be what it ought to be. It is probably true, nevertheless, that regular attendance indicates interest and reflects in a measure the quality of the teaching.

THE TEACHER TESTS THE CHILD

When we ask how we are to know whether our teaching is good, we are really thinking of only one thing. We are thinking of the pupils and whether something is happening in their lives that represents Christian growth.

There are always results of some kind that come from our teaching efforts, but the results are not always what the good teacher desires. Pupils are always learning something, but what they learn may not be the kind of thing that we would include among our Christian education aims. They may be learning how tiresome a class hour can be, or how irritated a teacher can become! Of course there will be teaching results, but our concern has to do with the kind of results.

Christian teaching is one of the chief tasks of the church,

perhaps the most important of all. It is not strange that Dr. Schisler [1] should make a case for the view that the church has no greater task than enlisting and training those who can really teach the Christian religion. If a church has a director of Christian education he or she will have many and varied responsibilities, but none is more important than that of securing those who will teach well and helping teachers to teach better. If a church has no employed director, it is not relieved of the responsibility of setting up a training program, looking toward teacher improvement. Every church needs to know its people, their abilities, interests, training and experience; if it does, it will be able to invite for the teaching task only the most competent. For the influence of the teacher may be very great. No one can ever tell how great this influence is to be, nor the point at which it will end. The teacher's influence is one of the indefinables of life.

To secure good teaching, we must make the environment as conducive to improvement as possible; we must teach as ably as we know how; and we must look for results. In the matter of securing the right environment, we work toward as satisfactory equipment as possible and we think of the general atmosphere and the spirit that pervades the school; for we know that it is easier to secure good results from our teaching when the environment is right. This, however, is not enough. Nor is it enough that our volunteers do an average teaching job and let it go at that. We must also keep an eye alert for results in the lives of the pupils themselves.

Some of these results we may be able to measure, but still there will be areas in which measurement is difficult. Even in these areas, however, we shall look for results and have opinions and convictions as to the nature of these results.

1. For one thing it is possible to know *whether the pupil has advanced in knowledge.* You may say that this is not the most important area in moral and religious education. Of course we grant any such contention, but it still remains true that the field

[1] Schisler, John Q., *Christian Teaching in the Churches,* Abingdon Press, 1954, p. 23.

of knowledge is important. It is one of the areas in which we look for growth and progress. We want our pupils to know and understand and appreciate the Bible as a whole, the life and teachings of Jesus, the story of the church, and other fields of study. There is real value in such understanding and appreciation. Not only does it have value in itself, but such knowledge is a stepping-stone into other areas of value; it is a tool that we use in Christian growth; it is a *sine qua non* for advance in the five fields that follow. Teaching is not good if it fails to give pupils adequate understandings, for their age, in this basic area of knowledge. Some of the so-called modern approaches in religious education are failing because they are failing at this point.

Too often volunteer teachers fail to make any effort to measure advance in knowledge. This is the easiest area in which to measure success and there are many ways in which this can be done. There is the time-honored examination; there is the True-False test; there is the Completion test; the Multiple-Choice test; there is the essay type or the method of report. But not the least important for the school with volunteer workers is the impression which the teacher gains as the weeks go by. An alert teacher can tell which members of the class have a reasonable amount of knowledge of the theme of study and some insight into its meaning.

2. We may also be concerned to note *whether pupils show Christian growth in their attitudes*. Here, for example, is the matter of reverence. Are these boys and girls reverent in worship? And, quite apart from services of worship, do they show a reverent attitude toward God, and life, and persons? Here also is the matter of one's attitude toward one's fellows: thoughtfulness, helpfulness, co-operation; or toward one's elders: politeness, respect, willingness to assist. One's attitude toward those of other racial, national, or cultural groups is a matter of deep concern to the church school teacher; is there growing respect for personality? or, on the other hand, is there a spirit of superiority and condescension or, at the other extreme, of cutting unkindness? Is the attitude of thankfulness a Thanksgiving Day pose or does it

permeate life increasingly through the year? Is the attitude of joy and of concern for others a thing to be talked about at the Christmas season or is it a growing reality in the lives of our pupils? We may make use of attitude tests which show how pupils say they feel about life situations, or we may observe their changing attitudes as we see them in their everyday life and behavior.

3. The church school teacher has a third concern — that teaching may find expression in the quality of *the pupil's everyday living*. The beatitudes are not only to be learned; they are to be lived. Learning them through living them is even more important than learning them through memorization. No one expects pupils to be transformed into faultless little saints because they go to Sunday School, but everyone has a right to expect some development and growth in the quality of their everyday living, as a result of the ministry of Christian education. And we have a right to expect this character growth to show itself — even though it be ever so slightly — in the home, at the school, in the church, or in times of free play. It is easy to observe during the hour at church school, but if one is to have an opinion as to everyday living in these other areas, one must know something about the pupils in these other areas.

4. Still another concern of the good teacher is that the pupil by doing some thinking of his own — under guidance — may *arrive at satisfying religious concepts and points of view* that will help him to build his Christian beliefs and his Christian philosophy of life. What is his concept of God? What is his thought of Jesus? What is his idea of prayer? How does he regard the church? Is he developing the beginnings, suited to his own age, of a Christian doctrine of man? Whatever one's ideas are in early life they will probably pass through many stages and changes, just as the ideas of every thinking adult change and grow through the years. We want children's ideas to be such as will help them; we want their beliefs to be of the kind that will not have to be unlearned or discarded as they mature; we want them to appreciate the developing idea of God through the Old Testament

and not be shocked by the thought that the God they worship once acted in ways that to us are nothing short of immoral or capricious. Many statements of belief are available, some with the backing of considerable authority and some with no claim to authority. Most of these statements have value if used in the right way. Certainly the wrong way is to suppose that boys and girls in the church school can arrive at satisfying religious points of view by the memorization of such creedal or catechetical statements. Such statements have value as points of reference, when graded to the pupil's age, but boys and girls who, under competent leadership, work out their own statements, accepting what is meaningful to them from the statements of others, will reach religious viewpoints that really satisfy. Church membership training classes need more of this approach. The point of this paragraph is that the good teacher looks for results in the form of religious points of view that are helpful at whatever stage of development the pupil may be.

5. The alert church school teacher looks for still another result: Are these pupils showing *a growing devotion to worthwhile causes in life,* suitable to their age and stage of development? The seven-year-old who denies herself an ice-cream cone in order to help a starving child across the sea is showing devotion to a cause suitable to her age. The ten-year-old who helps distribute bulletins for his church is manifesting a certain loyalty to his church. The thirteen-year-olds who, in their class discussion, take a position of honest concern for the cause of world peace or interracial justice are showing devotion to a cause that is rightly the concern of junior high boys and girls. One of the results for which the teacher looks is growing devotion to some significant cause in the world — the church itself, the worldwide mission of the church, some vital matter of social concern such as world-order or better race relations or a convinced position on the liquor issue. If we can see some results of this kind, our teaching, to that extent, has proved successful.

6. Every day we have decisions to make. A teacher may test the success of his teaching, also, by *the nature of the decisions his*

pupils make. It is not enough that young people be permitted to make their own decisions. The important point is that they make *informed* decisions; for this, good leadership is needed. Some of these they make in the classroom as they discuss pertinent questions or in the give and take of group life; these are easiest for the teacher to observe. Some decisions are made in the home, or at school, or at play. Some are decisions between honest and dishonest behavior. Some are decisions between selfishness and generosity. Some are choices between the way of love and the way of hate or reprisal. There comes a time when one makes a choice between identification with the church or refusal to do so; a time when one consciously chooses the Christian way of life as against a lower way of life. When young people are making up their minds as to their life work, consciously or unconsciously they are choosing between the motive of service and certain lower motives. Through all the church school years pupils are making decisions, some that we call little and some that we call big. To the extent that teachers can know these choices, to that extent can they measure in part the quality of their teaching.

The subject of this chapter is the most difficult question the church school teacher faces. Success in teaching is not measured by externals of attendance or behavior, but by progress at deeper levels. And the problem is complicated by the fact that even when we realize what these deeper levels are, we find it so difficult to measure the results. The volunteer teacher cannot go into the question of scientific measurement and character research. The volunteer teacher, however, can be on the lookout for results in such areas as those named above, some of which are often in danger of escaping our attention. There is much that we can sense that we may not measure with accuracy.

AS TEACHER I TEST MYSELF

To know whether your teaching is satisfactory, as a good teacher, test not only the pupil but also yourself. Look critically at yourself, your habits, your work, and take this look from many different angles.

In the following score-sheet thirteen separate areas are listed for the teacher's attention. An equally good list might well include fewer, or more, or different areas, but these at least are suggestive. Questions are given under each heading — fifty in all. To how many of these can you honestly answer " Yes "? Such a listing has value, chiefly, as it stimulates men and women to take stock, carefully, of their own activities and procedures and to select a few areas in which they are willing to go to work in order to improve their own teaching. These fifty questions may have value also as a basis for group discussion, and in such group discussion it may appear that in certain matters the viewpoint of the group differs from the implied viewpoint of the writer.

There is little value in trying to score somebody else, but in scoring ourselves there may be real value. If we do this with two points for each affirmative answer we must do it with the reservation that actually some items are far more important than others. The chief value of check-lists of this kind is always in their suggestiveness of emphases on which we need to concentrate our own efforts. This particular check-list will prove of no value unless it leads somebody, whose job is church school teaching, to take one or two points as areas in which to work, in an endeavor to improve the quality of that teaching.

LOOKING AT MYSELF AS A TEACHER

I. *The Teacher Is Also a Learner:*
   1. Do I use the workers' library? Have I read at least one book in the field of religious education this past year?
   2. Do I regularly read a Christian education magazine, denominational or interdenominational?
   3. If there is a leadership training institute in my own or a nearby community did I enroll in this past year's session?
   4. During the past three years have I attended at least one summer laboratory school or Religious Education Conference?

5. Can I be counted upon as a regular attendant at any conference, meeting or institute planned for teachers by my own church?

II. *The Good Teacher Makes Adequate Preparation:*

6. Do I make general preparation for teaching by studying the course as a whole in advance, and by looking up supplementary material?
7. Do I study each lesson, using both pupil's and teacher's books, and supplementing these when possible?
8. Is it my habit to begin my preparation well in advance — at least five days before the day I am to teach?

III. *As a Part of Advance Preparation the Good Teacher Makes a Written Lesson Plan:*

9. Do I write out a plan for each session I am to teach?
10. Do I regard this as a plan of the way I may proceed, knowing that circumstances may arise to make me decide to deviate from my written plan?
11. Is my plan sufficiently specific to indicate just how I may begin, how I may proceed, with sample questions, problems, and possible class activities, and how I may conclude the session?

IV. *The Teacher Approaches Sunday Morning With Confidence:*

12. Do I arrive at least fifteen minutes before the announced starting time?
13. Do I survey the situation to be sure that the room is orderly and neat, the ventilation satisfactory, coatracks and chairs where they should be, and so forth?
14. Do I make sure that all the " tools " I want to use are conveniently placed before starting time — such as pictures, books, materials for creative activities, chalk and eraser at the blackboard?
15. In making preparation before the session begins, do I enlist the co-operation of my pupils who arrive early so

that they feel themselves to be participants in the preparation and the planning?

V. *The Growing Teacher Is Always Trying to Improve in Skills:*

16. Do I practice telling stories so that I need not read them and may improve my telling techniques?

17. Do I study the techniques of group conversation and discussion-leading for the age which I teach, and endeavor by practice to improve myself in this art?

18. Do I study what others have done with pupils of the age of my class in the field of creative writing, and do I experiment in this field?

19. By attendance at a workshop, by study, and by practice, am I improving my own skill in such activities as note-book making, leading in informal dramatization, drawing, easel-painting, modeling in plasticene, making friezes, and so forth, so that I may be an informed and skillful leader of my children in the more effective use of such creative activities?

VI. *The Effective Teacher Realizes That the Pupil Must Be an Active Participant, Not Merely a Listener:*

20. Does my practice prove that I do not regard teaching as synonymous with telling or talking?

21. Is it my aim — and practice — to be a good listener and to draw out my pupils?

22. Although I help to steer procedure, do my pupils have a voice in determining their activities?

23. In practically every session do I devote at least part of the time to some form of creative activity (with a purpose) on the part of the pupils, or to discussion in which they participate?

24. Do I bring my pupils into the teaching task so that each one readily accepts an occasional assignment, and, if so, do I always call for it and make some use of it?

VII. *The Good Teacher Brings Variety Into the Procedure and Thus Introduces the Element of Surprise:*

25. In making my lesson plans do I vary the approach and the conclusion so that they are not always in the same general pattern?

26. Do I at times (especially with younger children) devote the whole session to some creative activity, which is really the lesson in another dress?

27. If my class customarily sits around the table do I vary the procedure and at times have the group somewhere other than "around the table"?

VIII. *The Effective Teacher Gives More Thought to the Pupils Than to Materials, Curriculum, or Any Other Matter:*

28. Do I know my pupils outside of class? Do I sometimes laugh with them? Do I know something of their recreation and social life?

29. Have I tried to find out what their school life is like, to become acquainted with their day-school teachers, and to inform myself as to their day-school curriculum?

30. Do I seek the co-operation of the pupils in the class program and, if I fail to secure co-operation, do I try to find the reason?

31. Would an outside observer describe me as one who respects the personality of every pupil?

IX. *The Successful Teacher Recognizes the Importance of His Own Personality and Personal Living:*

32. Do I have deep and genuine convictions in regard to the importance of teaching religion? If so, can I state them?

33. Does my record of church attendance and support of the work of the church prove my church loyalty?

34. In my actions, attitudes, and ideals do I seem to be, in a fair measure, an example of the kind of person held up in my teaching as the Christian ideal?

35. Am I sufficiently careful of my personal appearance so

that no lack in this respect will detract from the effectiveness of my work as a teacher?

X. *The Teacher Is a Member of a Team:*
   36. Do I work with others of the teaching staff and the Christian Education Committee in such a way that they think of me as a good co-operator, not as one who goes his own independent way?
   37. Am I regular both in my Sunday morning attendance and in attendance at workers' conferences or meetings of department teachers?

XI. *The Wise Teacher Recognizes the Importance of the Home:*
   38. Do I know the parents of my pupils personally, and have I seen them and their child in their own home? Am I able to interpret what happens in the class in the light of what I know of home life?
   39. Have I participated in parent-teacher meetings, and at such meetings have we made as much effort to secure suggestions from parents as to secure what some mistakenly call " their co-operation in our program "?
   40. Have I co-operated with others in an effort to enlist all the parents of my pupils in the activities and the fellowship of the church?
   41. Do I sometimes confer with parents in regard to their children's class work and their progress in the church school program?

XII. *The Thoughtful Teacher Is Critical of Self Even More Than of the Pupils When Faced With Non-co-operation and Disciplinary Problems:*
   42. Do I recognize disciplinary problems as more often due to poor teaching than to innate meanness in the pupil?
   43. Do I try to avoid disciplinary problems, not by rules and authority, but by building on pupils' interest, securing their co-operation, and enlisting them in purposeful activity?

44. Have I analyzed my experience to discover whether non-co-operation and problems of discipline appear more often when my lesson is poorly prepared and when I, myself, monopolize the time so that pupils have no place except that of mere listeners?

XIII. *The Good Teacher Always Looks for Results:*

45. Do I measure success, *in part*, by the pupil's growing knowledge and understanding of the subject matter of the course — the Bible, the history and work of the church, the life and teachings of Jesus, and so forth?

46. Do I measure success, *in part*, by the developing attitudes of my pupils — their growth in reverence, in thankfulness, in appreciation of other racial and cultural groups? Do I try to discover whether there is such growth?

47. Do I measure success, *in part*, by the quality of the pupil's everyday living — growth in the spirit of the beatitudes, and behavior at home, in school, at church and at play? Do I analyze the pupil's Christian living?

48. Do I measure success, *in part*, by the fact that my pupils are arriving at satisfying religious concepts — appropriate to their own stage of development — by their own thinking, under guidance, not by means of adult statements given them to accept?

49. Do I measure success, *in part*, as to whether the inevitable decisions of life are based increasingly on Christian motives — not only the decision for church membership and the Christian life at the appropriate time, but the simple decisions of life at every stage?

50. Do I measure success, *in part*, by my pupils' growing devotion to significant causes in ways that are suitable to their age and experience — the church, the world mission of the church, social concern, justice and human welfare — and do I try to determine whether my pupils show signs of such growth?

FOR FURTHER READING

GENERAL BOOKS ON BETTER TEACHING

Berkeley, James P. *You Can Teach.* Judson Press, 1941.

Chaplin, Dora P. *Children and Religion.* Charles Scribner's Sons, 1948.

Eakin, Mildred and Frank. *The Church School Teacher's Job.* Macmillan Co., 1949.

Gregory, John H. *The Seven Laws of Teaching.* Revised by William C. Bagley and Warren K. Layton. Baker Book House, 1954.

Highet, Gilbert. *The Art of Teaching.* Alfred A. Knopf, 1950.

Hoag, Victor. *It's Fun to Teach.* Morehouse Gorham Co., 1949 and 1953.

Jones, Mary Alice. *Guiding Children in Christian Growth.* Abingdon Press, 1949.

Lane, Howard and Beauchamp, Mary. *Human Relations in Teaching: the Dynamics of Helping Children Grow.* Prentice-Hall, Inc., 1955.

McLester, Frances C. *Teaching in the Church School.* Abingdon Press, 1940.

Vieth, Paul H. *How to Teach in the Church School.* Westminster Press, 1935.

Portfolio of Teaching Techniques. No. 1, a 60-minute refresher course for teachers; No. 2, Best practices in teaching and administration. 75 cents each. Arthur C. Croft Publications, New London, Conn.

MAGAZINES

Childhood Education, journal of the Association for Childhood Education International, 1200 15th Street, N. W., Washington, D. C. Monthly, September through May. $4.50 per year.

Children's Religion, a monthly magazine. Pilgrim Press.

International Journal of Religious Education, a monthly magazine. National Council of Churches, 475 Riverside Drive, New York 27, N. Y. $4.00 per year.

BASIC TOOLS FOR THE TEACHER

The Bible: Revised Standard Version and other translations.

A Bible dictionary such as *Harper's Bible Dictionary*, Madeleine S. and J. Lane Miller. Harper & Bros., 1952.

A Bible concordance such as *Analytical Concordance to the Bible*, Robert Young, Funk & Wagnalls, 1953.

A Bible commentary: *The Interpreter's Bible* (twelve volumes, $89.50; single volume, $8.75), Abingdon Press, or *Abingdon Bible Commentary*, one volume.

The Westminster Historical Atlas to the Bible, ed. Wright and Filson, Westminster Press, 1945.

Encyclopedia of Child Care and Guidance. Doubleday & Co., 1954.

EDUCATIONAL ACTIVITIES, STORY TELLING, GROUP DISCUSSION

Brown, Jeanette Perkins. *The Storyteller in Religious Education*. Pilgrim Press, 1951.

Keiser, Armilda D. *Here's How and When*. Friendship Press, 1952.

Lobingier, Elizabeth M. *Activities in Child Education*. Pilgrim Press, 1950.

Strauss, Bert and Frances. *New Ways to Better Meetings*. Viking Press, 1951.

Trecker, Harleigh B. and Audrey R. *How to Work with Groups*. Whiteside, Inc., 1952.

Welker, Edith F. *Friends with All the World*. Friendship Press, 1954.

DISCIPLINE

Baruch, Dorothy W. *New Ways in Discipline*. McGraw-Hill Book Co., 1949.

Hymes, James L., Jr. *Behavior and Misbehavior: a Teacher's Guide to Action*. Prentice-Hall, Inc., 1955.

Murray, Janet P. and Clyde E. *Guide Lines for Group Leaders*. Whiteside, Inc., 1954.

VISUAL RESOURCES

Hockman, W. S. *Projected Visual Aids in the Church*. Pilgrim Press, 1947.

Tower, Howard E. *Church Use of Audio-Visuals*. Abingdon Press, 1950.

Audio-Visual Resource Guide for Use in Religious Education. National Council of Churches.

TEACHING AT VARIOUS AGE LEVELS

Cummings, Oliver DeW. *Guiding Youth in Christian Growth*. Judson Press, 1954.

Griffiths, Louise B. *The Teacher and Young Teens*. Bethany Press, 1954.

Hill, Dorothy LeCroix. *Working with Juniors at Church*. Abingdon Press, 1955.

Knowles, Malcolm S. *Informal Adult Education*. Association Press, 1950.

Roorbach, Rosemary K. *Religion in the Kindergarten*. Harper & Bros., 1952.

Smither, Ethel L. *Primary Children Learn at Church*. Abingdon Press, 1944.

Venable, Mary E. *The Church School Nursery Class*. Pilgrim Press, 1954.

Wills, Clarice D. and Stegeman, William H. *Living in the Kindergarten*. Follett Publishing Co., 1951.

INDEX

[153]